Oil Painting Medic

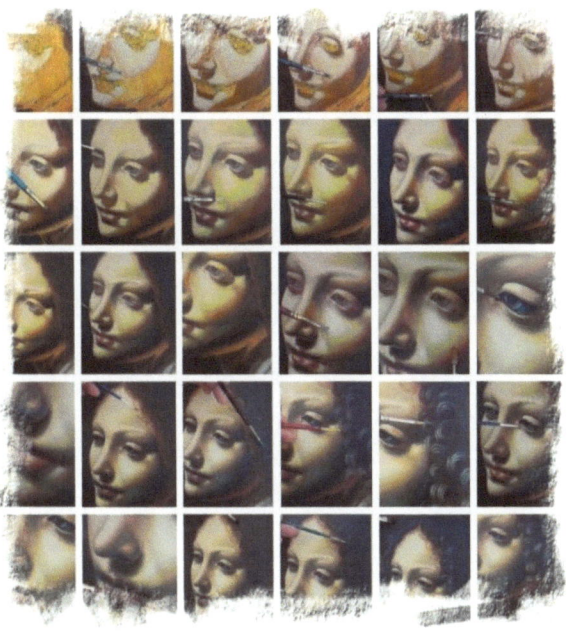

Oil Painting the Angel within Da Vinci's the Virgin of the Rocks
Unleash the Right Brain to Paint the Three-quarter Portrait View

Rachel Shirley

ISBN-13:978-1535421935
ISBN-10:1535421932

First Published in 2016 by Rachel Shirley

To my family

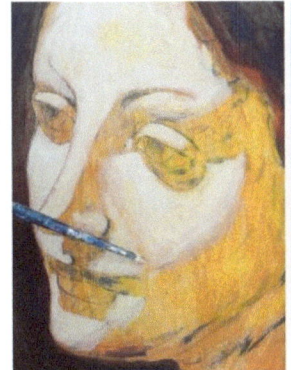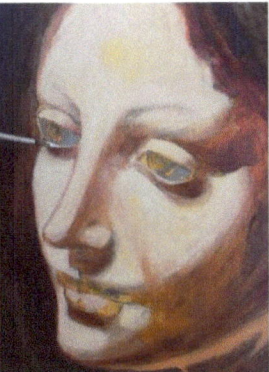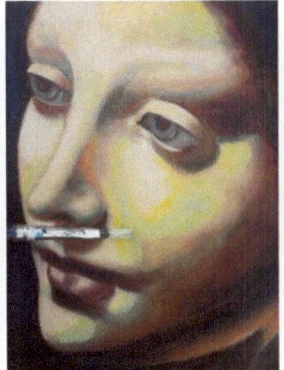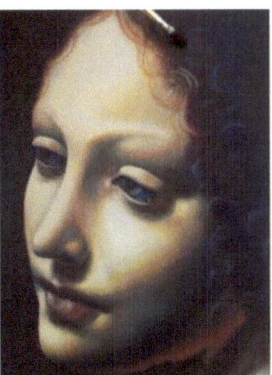

Contents

Introduction

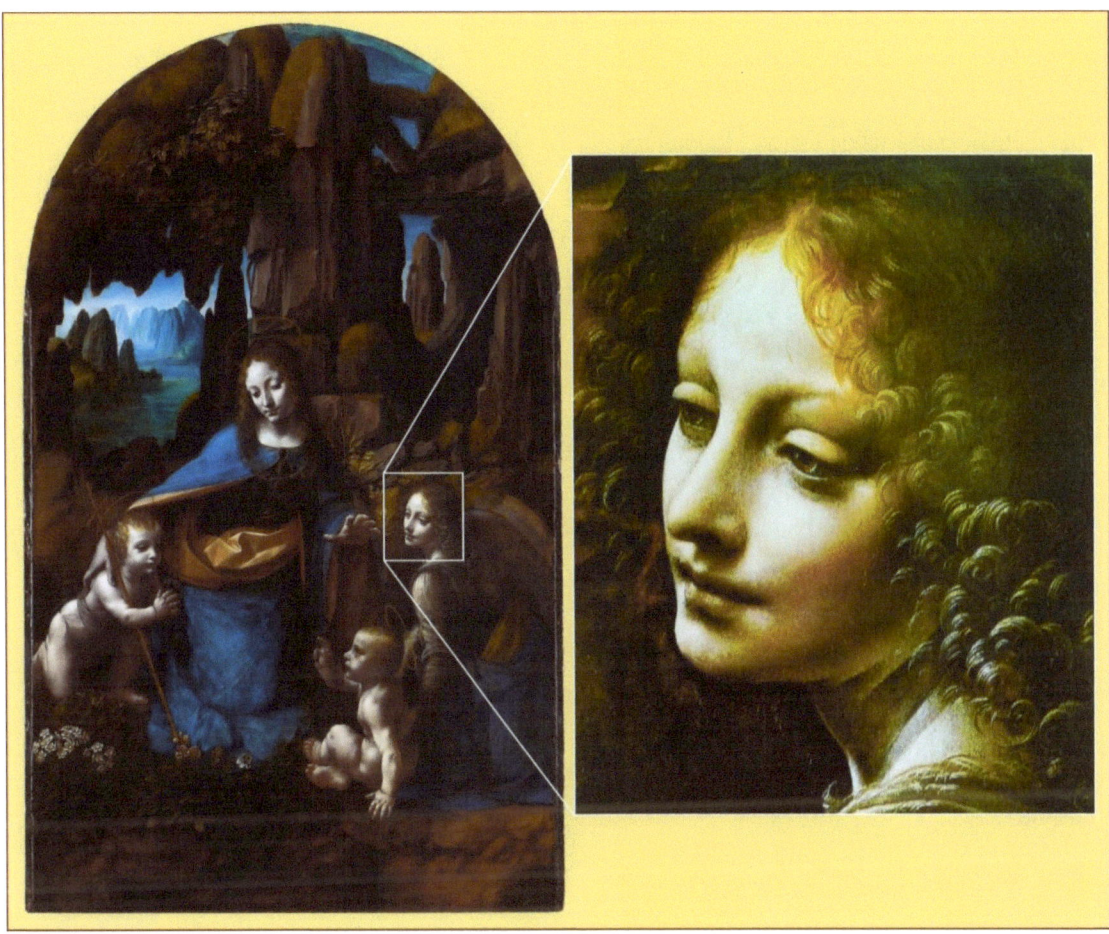

PAINTING A PORTRAIT in three-quarter view poses challenges not encountered when painting a portrait face-on or in profile. This can be seen within the subject of this book: the mysterious angel located to the right of Leonardo da Vinci's *The Virgin of the Rocks,* completed in 1508 (pictured above).

A close-up view of the angel brings clarity to the task at hand. The face from such an angle makes this subject matter ideal for the artist wishing to delve into the challenging realms of portraiture.

Elements to explore within this book are several: namely expressing subtle colour shifts with the ebbing planes of the face, dissolving highlights into shadow via *sfumato* technique (explained in a moment), suggesting the sleek curls of the hair, capturing the translucency of the angel's eyes and the application of high detail in the style of the early Renaissance period. For this reason, such a project requires a certain amount of dedication and commitment.

To this end, this book describes in detail how this painting has been completed, beginning with the art materials required, challenges to consider and laying down the foundations for the oil painting. This is followed by step by step images accompanied by detailed instructions, thus creating the perfect portrait painter's workout.

But before embarking upon this oil painting, let's learn a little more about the artist and this masterpiece.

Leonardo's other Masterpiece

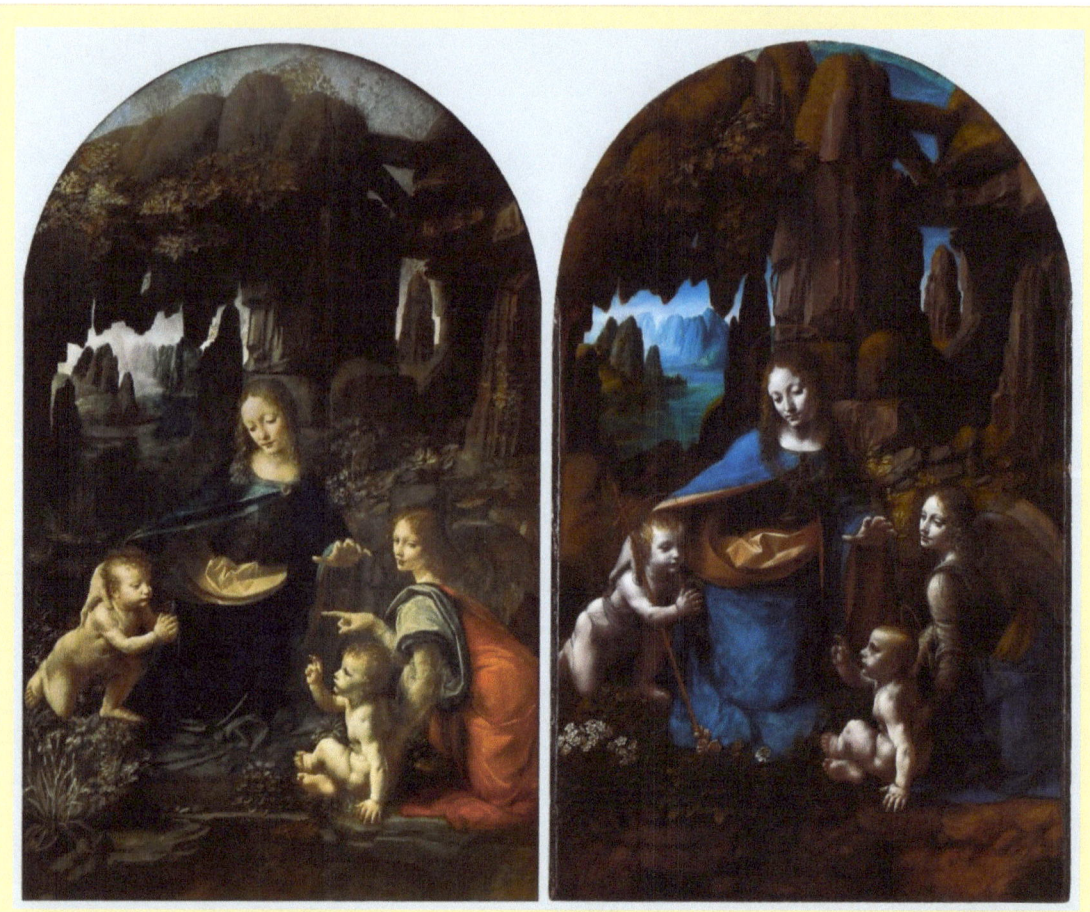

(**Left**) Leonardo da Vinci's first rendition of *the Virgin of the Rocks*, begun around 1483 and which is located in the Louvre, Paris (199 cm×122 cm). (**Right**) Da Vinci's later version was begun around 1508 and which is located in the National Gallery, London (189.5 cm×120 cm).
As can be seen from the two images, his later version evidences deeper tonal values, bordering upon *chiaroscuro* – (meaning 'bright-dark') and a more polished finish.

In contrast to Leonardo da Vinci's *the Mona Lisa,* housed within the Louvre in Paris, few may notice his other masterpiece not far away. *The Virgin of the Rocks (*sometimes referred to as *the Madonna of the Rocks)*. This painting in fact forms the earlier version of two paintings, the latter of which is housed within the National Gallery, London and to which forms the focus of this book.

But this relatively obscure painting possesses astonishing qualities deserving more than a pause or a passing glance. Most striking are the depth of tones of the figures, particularly of the latter version. The two images above provide a comparison between the two. The observer may notice a few differences, such as the colour of Mary's gown, the inclusion of haloes, a cross and the omission of the angel's pointing finger.

Highlights and darks within the figures reside close by, yet there are few discernible lines. Creating such a smooth transition between tones is known as *sfumato*, a pioneering technique of the Renaissance period and to which Da Vinci was credited. It is an Italian word derived from *sfumare*, which means 'like smoke'.

Sfumato of the Mona Lisa versus the Angel

Sfumato is chiefly associated with Da Vinci's *the Mona Lisa*, where the effects are indeed ethereal, like smoke.

Sfumato effects can be seen in the angel, but, having also painted *the Mona Lisa* (outlined in my other art instruction book), I have noticed vital differences in approach between the two portraits, albeit subtle.

Firstly there are additional hues to the customary browns of *the Mona Lisa*. In the angel, we can see bands of definite hues across the cheek, temple and chin, including blues, crimsons and even greens (explored in more depth in stage 4). Secondly, a linear aspect can be seen on the angel's face, particularly around the nose and the eyes. Lines are somewhat lacking in *the Mona Lisa*.

The lighting is also more dramatic, resonating of *chiaroscuro*, an Italian word meaning 'light dark' and which was further developed by Caravaggio.

The grotto setting behind the angel describes everything that *sfumato* is not: linear and full of ridges and harsh textures. In this way, a distinction between the figures and the setting is set up.

The grouping has been delicately orchestrated, creating balance and a feeling of serenity. We see the Madonna, looking down towards the adoring John the Baptist. The Christ Child returns his cousin's gaze as he points emphatically to the sky. In the latter depiction, all three figures bear haloes, leaving little doubt as to the theme of this painting and of their identities.

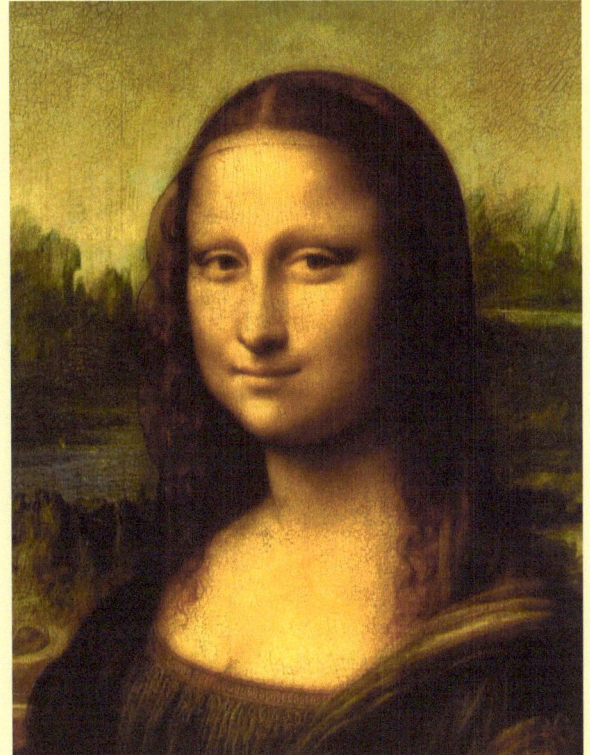

As can be seen here, *sfumato* effects of *the Mona Lisa* comprise mostly tobacco-hues of browns and greys with little colour.

Why the Painting Existed

When one considers that Leonardo was a serial non-finisher of commissions and in fact completed few paintings in his lifetime, it would seem odd that he painted *the Virgin of the Rocks* twice. Madonna and child themes had indeed obsessed Da Vinci, but no sooner had he solved the compositional problem, would he lose interest and move onto another project. Between the launch of this painting and its completion, Da Vinci had involved himself in many projects, including *The Last Supper* (c1498) and *The Mona Lisa* (c1504). He showed a obsession with countless subject matter: botany, human anatomy, spatial puzzles and others.

For this reason, his conceptual drawings far outweigh the quantity of his paintings.

The church of San Fransecso Grande in Milan had originally commissioned Da Vinci to paint *the Virgin of the Rocks* to provide the central segment to an altarpiece in 1483. The deadline was to be seven months. Twenty-five years later, Da Vinci delivered. A monetary dispute was the reason for the delay.

Two other panels showing an angel playing musical instruments was to flank the central altarpiece, but which now are also located at the National Gallery. Some argue the latter version had involved the hand of studio aids.

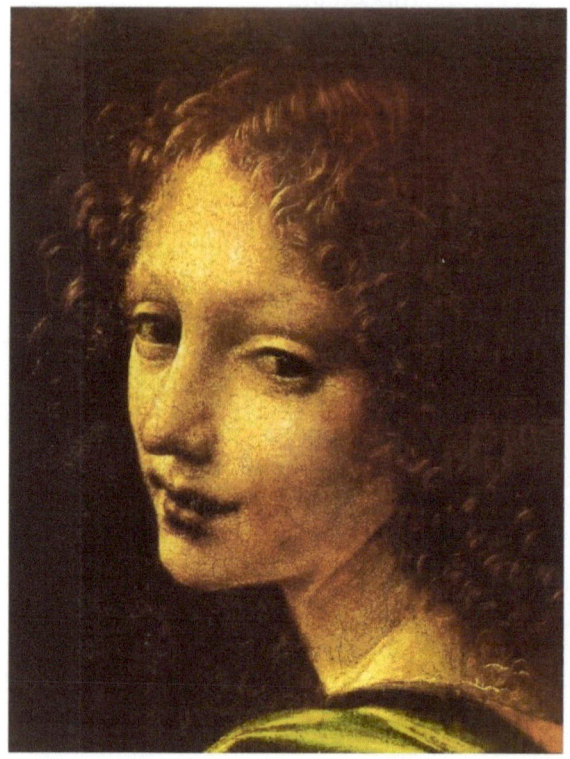 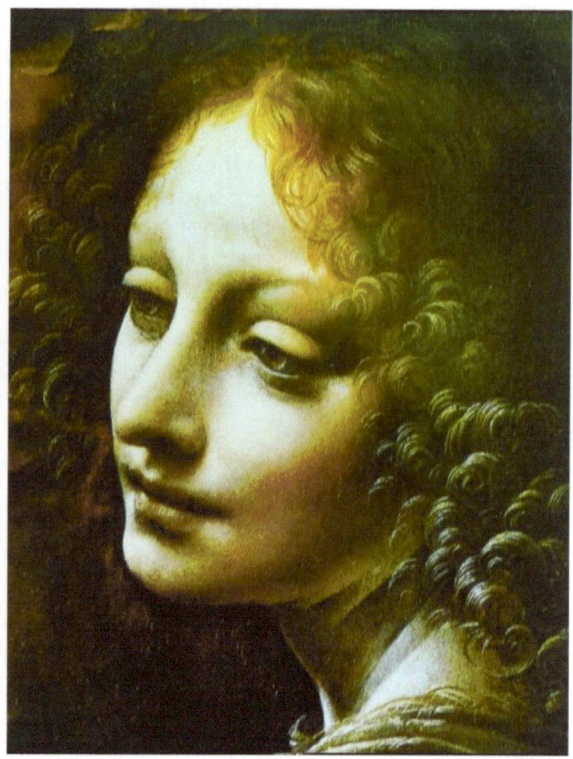

Close-up views of the angel. (**Left**) the earlier version. Her gaze is directed over her shoulder. Soft, *sfumato* effects are evident but bear monochromic hues, mainly sepias and umbers, echoing the approach used within *the Mona Lisa*. (**Right**) the later version 25 years later. As can be seen here, Da Vinci's *sfumato* technique has been refined and her gaze is directed ahead. Notice higher contrasts in light and shadow along with subtle hues within the twilight.

But it is the angel gazing across, lost in thought that demonstrates Leonardo's striking achievement in rendition – *sfumato* at its most refined. Notice the delicate yet deep shadows describing her features, reflected light across the jaw-line and bands of colour where light and shadow meet. Notice also selective use of line.

In many ways, painting the angel's face poses challenges not encountered in *the Mona Lisa* in that there are colours to consider as well as lines. A heavy approach regarding hue could cause a garish outcome; a diffident approach could result in a washed-out rendition.

So how does the artist tackle such a challenge as painting the angel within *the Virgin of the Rocks*? Well, the secret is to take the painting one step at a time.

The first section of this book looks at the preparatory stages of the painting, which forms a vital component to a successful rendition. This includes the materials required, how to reap the benefits of oils and learning more about *sfumato* technique. But more importantly, we will also look at ways of subduing the left brain during the painting's execution, as even the best art materials cannot overcome a poor underdrawing. But as can be seen in stage 2 of this book, strategies can be used to overcome this problem.

This is followed by the main body of the book, which provides numerous images, each with in depth step-by-step instructions on each stage of the oil painting process. The final chapter looks at self-assessment, including ways in which to improve and develop in future portrait painting.

Not Just Sfumato

Leonardo's angel requires several oil painting techniques to capture the effects evident, but *sfumato* forms a chief application.

Briefly, *sfumato* is an Italian word from *'sfumare'*, meaning to evaporate like smoke. The highlights on the angel's face do indeed seem to evaporate into shadow. In these areas, the outline of the face cannot be pinned down.

However we can also see definite outlines around the nose and the right side of the face, as well as wispy effects around the hair and high detail on the eyes. Achieving these effects requires soft brushing, blending, smudging, glazing, delineating and more.

Each technique is explored when the need arises. However, the preparatory stage to this painting is vital as it forms the foundation onto which the portrait can develop successfully. A state of mind is also needed. Rather than complete the painting in one go, several sessions are required.

In this case, the painting was completed within a week. Five sessions of between one to two hours was practiced here, but every artist will differ in approach. What is vital is not to over-tax oneself over hours. An achievable goal is the best way to go. This means the underdrawing can be completed on one day; the foundation glaze on another. The oil paint can then be applied when feeling most up to the challenge. A fresh eye will help resolve problems rather than rushing to the end.

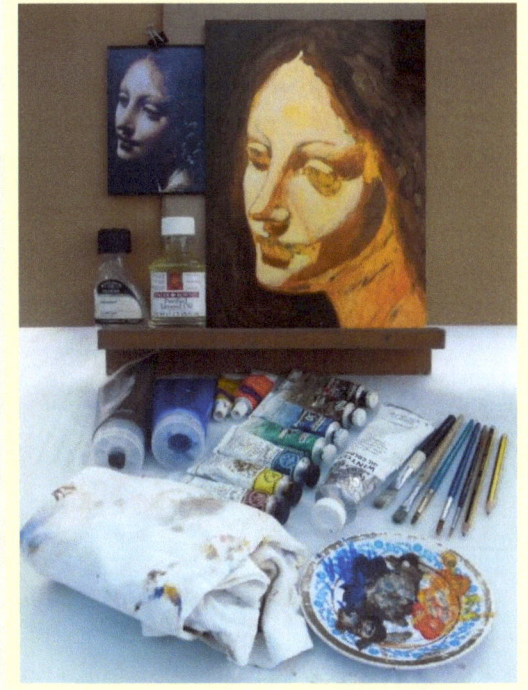

Art materials required to complete this painting: primed panel, acrylic paints, oil pigments, artist solvent, linseed oil, sables, bristles, rags and a mixing palette.

The Portraitist's Art Kit

The materials used in this painting can be found in every art shop and are not costly or unwieldy. I used brown, blue, yellow and red acrylic paint in order to inject various colour temperatures into the upper paint layers. Oil pigments used include: titanium white, cadmium yellow, alizarin crimson, burnt sienna, burnt umber, pthalo blue and viridian green.

Ready-sized art panels can be purchased from any art shop, but I prepare my own by applying two coasts of acrylic gesso size over a piece of MDF measuring 10x12in. Between each coat, I lightly sanded the surface to attain extra smoothness. The artist may use fine-stretched canvas, but is worth bearing in mind that Leonardo worked on panel.

The weave would also make fine detail more difficult to express.

An assortment of oil painting brushes were used to achieve the various effects described in this book. They need not be brand new or of the highest quality. In fact, I prefer my brushes to be a little worn and rounded.

Stiff ox hair brushes are invaluable for the *sfumato* effects and for blocking in large areas of paint. Fine sables are suitable for expressing detail.

In summary, sable nos. 3, 6 and 10 rounds have been used for soft brushing and detail (herein referred to as fine, medium and wide); and 6, 10 and 12 flat or filbert ox hair bristles were used for blocking in large areas of paint, as well as shading (referred to as fine, medium and wide bristles). Also used are linseed oil and odorless artist spirits.

I used an old china plate as my mixing palette, but any non-porous surface will do, such as old Tupperware lids or Clingfilm stretched over a piece of board via bulldog clips. The used palette can easily be folded into itself and disposed of without having to use spirits. Other art materials include soft HB pencils, rags, used pots and a means with which to transfer the image onto panel, which might be a free hand, tracing paper or an enlarger.

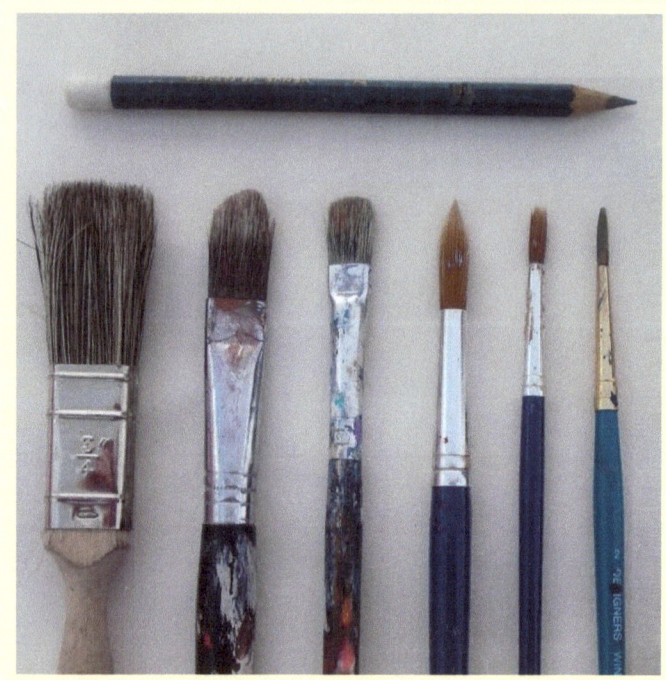

Implements used for the painting: A soft pencil, wide, medium and fine flat bristles; wide, medium and fine round sables.

The Angel Step by Step

Visual vigilance and the right frame of mind are needed for this painting, which is why this book is divided into 6 stages:

- **Stage 1**: The challenges ahead.
- **Stage 2**: Underpinning the painting
- **Stage 3**: The foundation glaze.
- **Stage 4**: Bands of colour.
- **Stage 5**: Shadow refinements.
- **Stage 6**: Framing the face

The painting was completed in separate stages, so there is no need to work for hours at a time. Each stage is explained fully, along with the art technique involved. Of course, the great thing about oils is that they remain workable for hours. But this also means getting the consistency right. On the latter stages of the painting, the oil paint was applied quite neat, which means going easy on the linseed oil. *Sfumato* effects are impossible to achieve if the paint consistency is too thin or runny, as all control will be lost. On the other hand, detail requires a fine sable and little linseed oil to help the paint flow, as stage 6 will show. As will be seen, *sfumato* and detail application are opposites when it comes to technique.

As this project is quite challenging, postponing for another day might be necessary if something refuses to work out. A fresh mind and eye is more likely to solve problems. More about challenges that might be encountered is covered in the following section.

Painting the Angel: an Overview

Great depth of colour and tone is made achievable by applying the oil paint in layers, known as 'glazes'. Some of the old masters applied up to 10 glazes or more. This project requires 4 oil glazes. But this does not mean that every glaze should cover the entire painting, only select areas.

The slow drying time of oils means that modifications can be made at leisure, essential for blending and shading.

Some oil pigments thicken quicker than others. Burnt umber for instance begins to oxidize within a few hours, which means it will attain quite a crayon-like consistency towards the end of the session. This is ideal for *sfumato* shading.

Alizarin crimson and burnt sienna on the other hand dries more slowly, and by comparison is quite oily. Mixing the two will provide extra flow to the paint without having to add mediums. This is vital for a successful rendition of Leonardo's angel.

The Three-Quarter Dilemma

BEFORE BEGINNING the oil painting, a dilemma may require resolving regarding the artist's brain, and this is due to the three-quarter view of the angel's face.

Put simply, we see the world in two conflicting ways. The first is to label things, to edit reality in order to make sense of the world. In the case of the human head, the left brain sees the nose as a nub-ended projection situated at the centre of the face and which has two nostrils. The eyes are two almond-shaped forms framed by eyelids, and the mouth comprises two slender lips, the upper giving way to a Cupid's bow. All have definite elements in common and to which come under these labels. This figurative view of the world is perhaps due to our language centre, which happens to be located within the left hemisphere.

The features of the face can easily be illustrated as symbols when viewed front-on or in profile. But the three-quarter view presents a visual enigma that cannot be so easily resolved. Guesswork can slip into the artwork, which can ruin the portrait. These pitfalls may seem obvious and over-simplistic, but can sneak into the painting in the most subtle of ways.

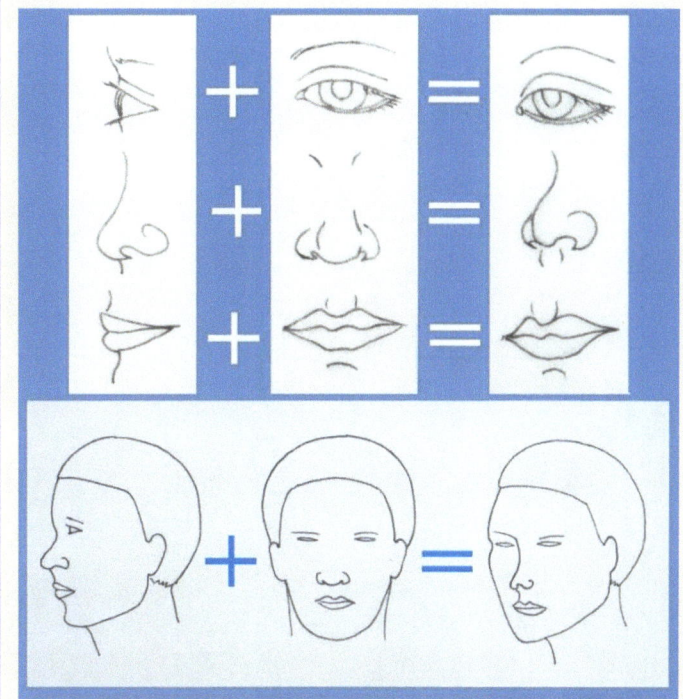

Top: the facial features illustrated as symbols. Above: The left-brained dilemma of the portrait in three-quarter view. The rendition may contain elements of the profile and frontal view, causing a skewed outcome, as seen here.

The Left Brain's Equations and Symbols

The illustration shows the left brain's tendency to solve visual enigmas by taking an overly-pragmatic view. Here, we can see symbols often used to represent the facial features: in profile view, face-on and in three-quarter view. This illustrates the left brain's tendency to find a solution to a visual enigma, whether or not the answer to the puzzle represents reality. A skewed appearance to a face in three-quarter view may possess features exhibiting frontal and/or profile view. Giving in to such a left-brained dogma must be avoided.

This portrait painting exercise permits little scope for rendering the facial features in such a linear or symbolic way. However, the left-brained view may persevere in the most subtle of ways, insisting upon rules and making assumptions.

The artist needs to be extra vigilant of such elements within the artwork and to look at the painting with a purely open, almost child-like way.

Which brings me to the second way of seeing the world: from the right-brain.

The right brain is silent, seeing things without labels, symbols or assumptions, but as they actually are: abstract shadow-shapes and lines that come together to *look* like a nose, a mouth or an eye.

Tapping into this way of seeing regarding shading and colour-use is not difficult to do, as will be seen next.

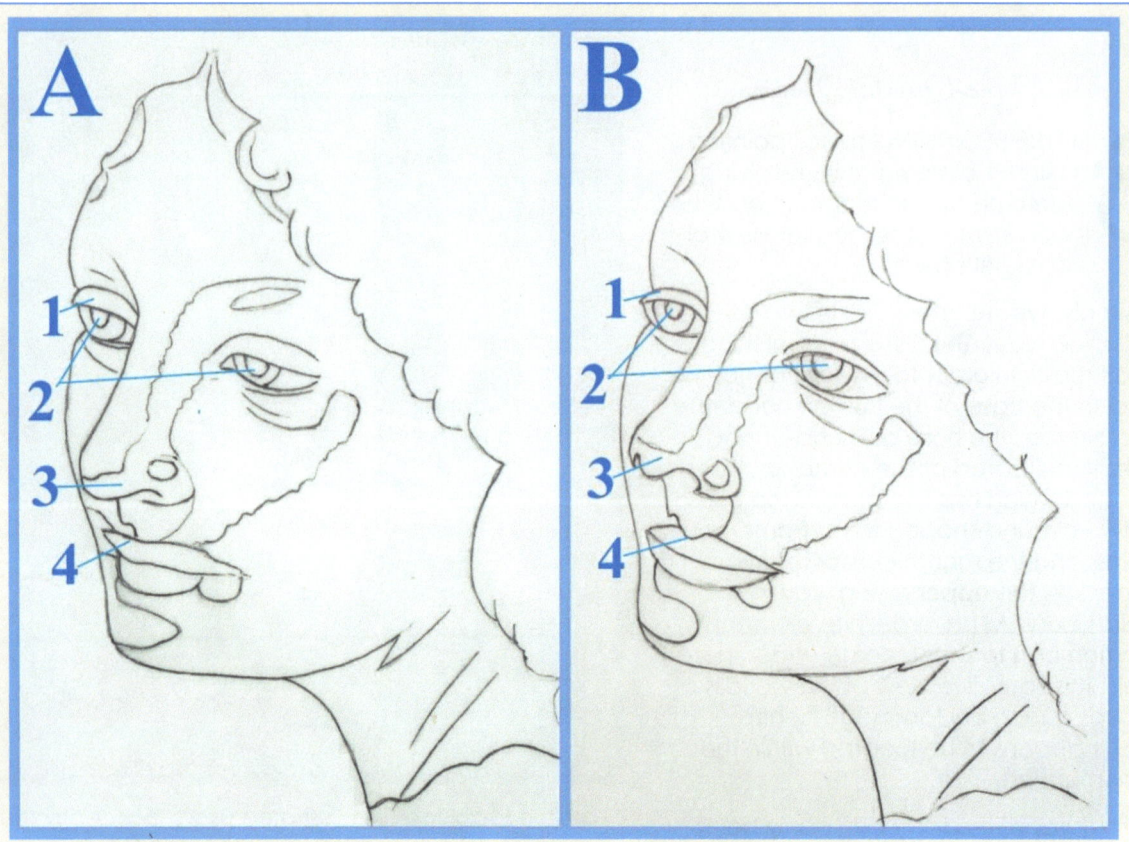

Issues that can arise when drawing a portrait in three-quarter view. **A** represents an accurate drawing. **B** illustrates common drawing errors that can be inherited within the paint layer.

Problems with Drawing the Three-quarter View

Awareness of the pitfalls to look out for form part of the project, as we have already seen, regarding the left side of the brain that edits the world by making assumptions and reducing objects to symbols and formulas. This section looks as other problems to watch out for.

Problems within a painting can be traced back to the underdrawing. Take a look at **A**: an accurate drawing and **B**: showing drawing errors.

As discussed earlier, the left brain can sneak into the painting in numerous ways, making assumptions and filling in gaps when the artist forgets to 'look' at the visual resource. Drawing by memory is the enemy of realism and should be avoided. The dilemma of the three-quarter portrait view can also exacerbate the problem, as the left brain likes rules But here, the face is not full-frontal, nor in profile.

For some, this can pose an unsolvable puzzle, causing the artist to resort to memory or by 'what is known' about the human head. Watch out for the following:

1 Expressing the eyes as almond shapes or a compromise between such symbols and what is evident.

2 The pupils provide the chief focus of the painting, so ensure both are similar in size and the correct quantity is exposed beneath the eyelids.

3 Expressing the furthest nub of the nose when none can be seen. This might occur due to the left brain insisting that the nose has two nostrils and two sides, and therefore both should be visible.

4 Insisting upon a Cupid's bow and/or placing it almost central of the upper lip in spite of the feature's orientation.

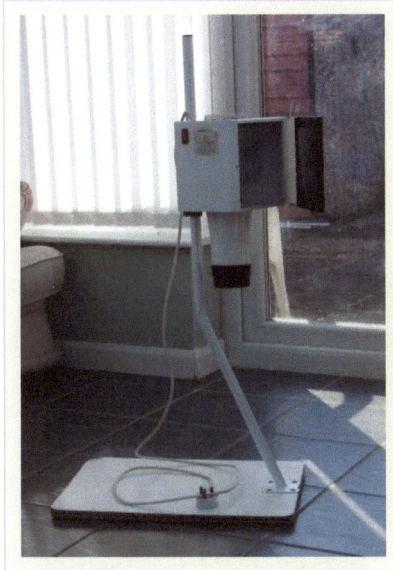

Alternative to Freehand Drawing

Of course, a drawing aid might be preferable to sketching freehand. Several methods can be used, including scaling up from a grid, tracing the drawing and using an enlarger. All are ideal, but will not guard against the left brain's dogma sneaking into the painting in the most subtle of ways. Working on top of an accurate drawing will also not guarantee that the painting will not fall foul of assumptions as just described. Outlines can never truly illustrate the meeting of light and shadow, only provide a rough estimation. Where there are gaps, the left brain will tend to fill it in.

The best way to approach the project is to banish every assumption along with what is 'known' during the *entire* project from the drawing stage and throughout the painting. Observe Leonardo's angel as a series of abstract shapes and contours without symbols, equations or assumptions.

Forestalling the left brain and unleashing the right is also vital when it comes to rendering tones.

The Left-Brained System of Expressing Tones

The sketch represents issues that can arise whilst keying in tones during the painting process.

1 Outlines of the hair are harsh, lacking any variation in tone.

2 Large, flat areas of highlight lack subtle shading to illustrate form.

3 A linear approach to eyebrows.

4 Shadows illustrated in a patchy way as though shapes in isolation.

5 Knowledge of the eyeballs being white interfering with judging their true tonal value, being quite dark.

6 Nose being perceived as a tubular shape causing the simplified rendition of side shading, without variation.

7 Shadow beneath the nose is too dark, causing an unwanted focal point.

8 Outlines illustrated on lips when none can be seen on the painting.

9 Shading on the cheek is progressively darker without reflected light.

10 Folds on the neck are illustrated in a linear fashion.

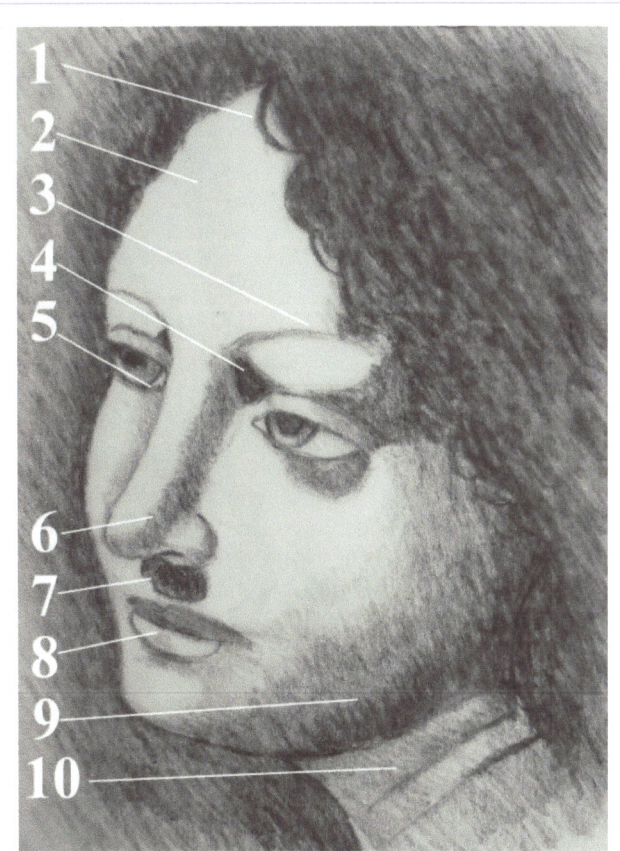

Issues with expressing tones on the three-quarter portrait.

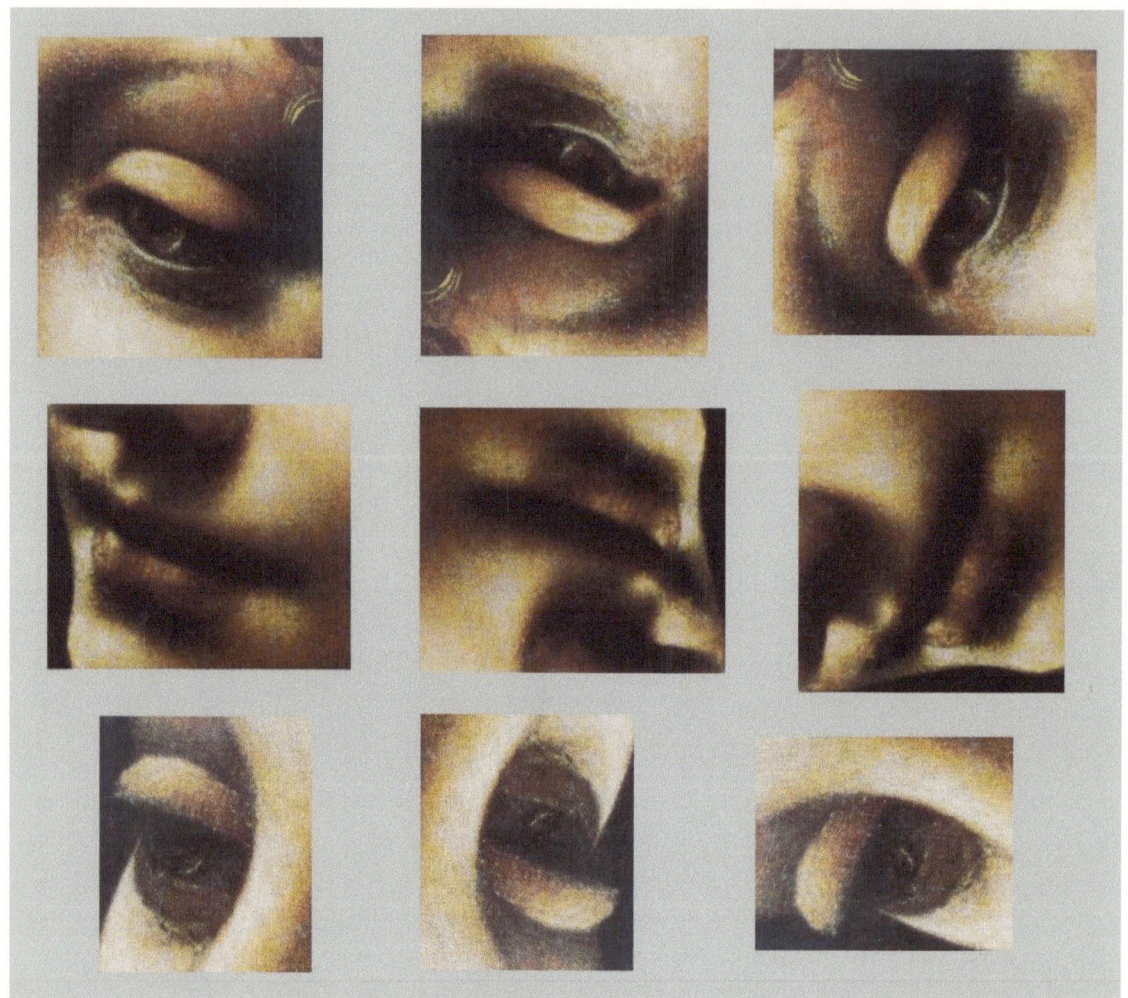

Rendering a feature from an unfamiliar orientation can forestall assumptions and create a fresh view.

A high visual awareness, as found within the right side of the brain can be developed by turning the painting and the visual resource upside down or on its side. As can be seen in these images, a facial feature will look very different when orientated in various ways to the point where it can almost be unrecognizable. Rendering a feature into abstract shapes will mute the left brain, as there are no rules to follow. This will permit a more truthful rendition of the portrait.

Consider the following regarding line, colour and shape:

1 The nature of outlines, if any can be seen. Is it sharp, soft, does it vary along the way; what is its thickness, and does it vanish at certain points?

2 The nature of tonal shapes. What is the degree to which it fades into another shape; what is its colour and tonality?

3 The nature of light and shade. What is the degree to which the shadows shift into highlight and vice versa? Does is shift in colour?

4 Semblance of shadow-shapes to objects. For example, does an area of colour resemble a crescent moon, a hammer, a trilby hat or a combination of two objects?

14

The Correct Tonal Key

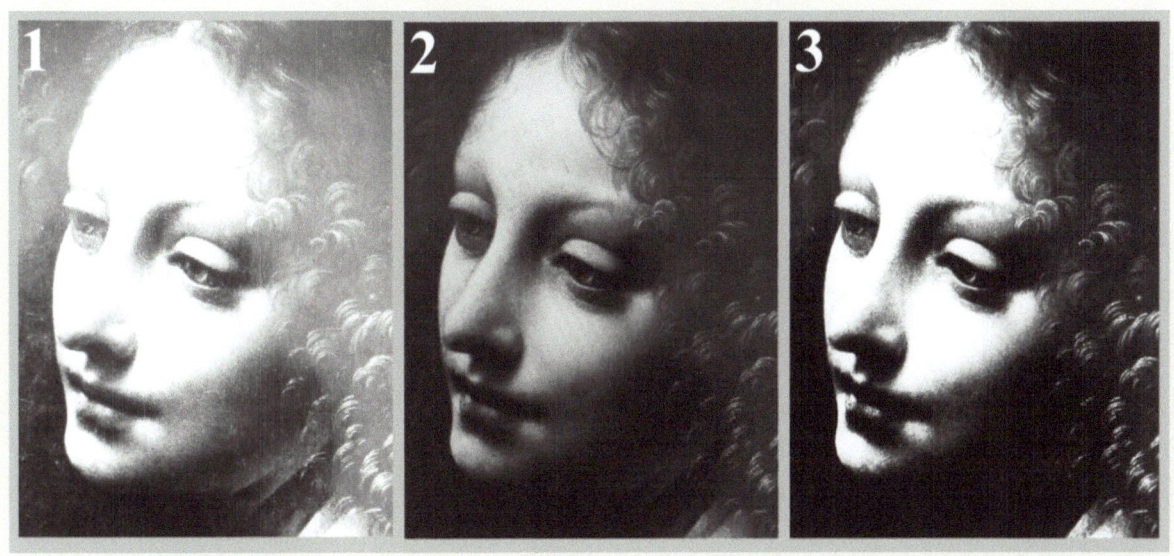

The tonal key of an image. **1** is too pale, describing a high tonal key. **2** is too dark, describing low tonal key. **3** has few mid-tones, having high contrast. None of these situations is ideal for the portrait painting.

A further challenge of painting the angel is getting the tonal key right. The tonal key describes how pale or dark the overall tones are on an image, as can be seen. Imbalances in tones within a painting can rob the subject matter of any form or suggestion of texture. Achieving tonal balance also means examining how one area relates to another.

The Correct Tonality of a Painting

1. This image has a high tonal key, exhibiting lots of pales and few darks. Painting straight onto a white primed art surface can cause a false impression as to the tonality of the initial paint layer which can have a knock-on effect throughout the entire painting. The result is a pale painting.

The answer is to apply a dilute layer of paint to kill the whiteness of the painting surface. Such a wash is known as the *imprimatura* or an underglaze, explored in the following section.

2. This image has a low key, possessing darker tones. The highlights appear quite muted and detail is lost within shadows. An underexposed photograph may have a similar look.

3. This image possesses high contrast. Heavy shadows and bleached-out highlights permit little mid-tone. The face looks flat, with little form.

None of these situations is desirable in the painting. This means getting the right overall tonal key.

Not too pale, not too dark and not with high contrast but with plenty of mid-tones.

Be sure to express all tonal values from very pale to very dark and everything in between.

These points might seem obvious but can be overlooked when obsessing over one area of the painting. View light and shadow as tonal shapes with various edges. Some will be softer or steeper than others.

Observe how one tonal area relates with another. View tonal shapes as a jigsaw with soft or harsh edges that fit together to form a painting.

Ask the serial question: how does one area relate to another? Is it darker, softer, how does tones veer from one value to another? Be careful not to express lines that are imagined or to sit too close to the painting, depriving an overall view.

A perfect balance between tonal values is the ideal outcome.

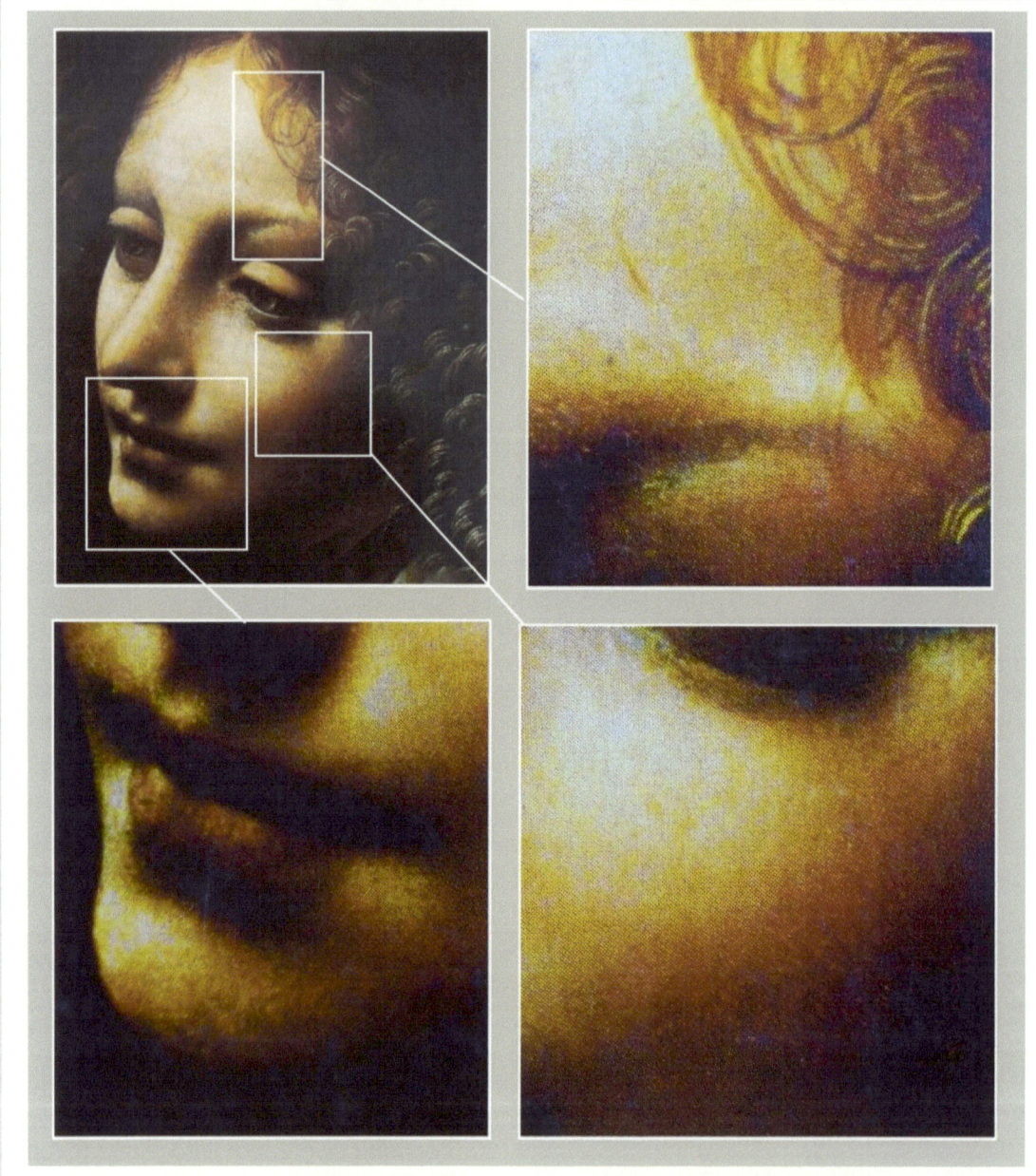

These colour-enhanced images show bands of colours where light and shadow meet.

The final element to be aware of with the angel's face is the bands of colour at the junction of where light and shadow meet. The three enlarged images have been colour-enhanced to illustrate this point. Here, we can see subtle but definite hues absent within *the Mona Lisa.*

Yellows, ochres, crimsons and even a tinge of green can be perceived in places. The highlights give way to blues and then to browns. Expressing such bold colours requires a degree of bravery in the painting process but is worth it.

With the challenges set out, it is time to begin the painting.

Stage 2: Underpinning the Painting

SOME ARTISTS might be happy to begin the oil painting without an underdrawing, which is fine if possessing sufficient confidence, but is not always necessary. Thorough preparation is vital for a successful painting. This is why I would recommend the view that the preparatory stage is a project in itself. Set aside a separate day for completing the drawing and with resolving niggles, such as those described within the previous section before laying paint onto board.

Plot every line as accurately as possible and ensure the head occupies a good portion of the art board. As can be seen here, I have placed the angel's head slightly to the right of the art surface, providing a little breathing space in the direction of her gaze. The background occupies roughly one-tenth of the total art surface.

Using the eraser is not a sin and it doesn't matter if the drawing displays numerous corrections. Work pale with a soft pencil until assured of accuracy. Don't view visual features as isolated entities, but as part of a whole. Check how one feature relates to another regarding size orientation and coordinate. Stand back to get an overall view and examine the drawing upside down to expose possible drawing errors. The drawing need not be neat or beautiful, as the lines will be concealed anyway. Simply aim for accuracy.

Shadow Boundaries

As can be seen here, not every feature of the face can be expressed as a line. The meeting of light and dark on the cheekbone and temple, for example can at best be indicated by a few soft strokes. Express lines only where they can be seen, such as around the eyes, bridge of the nose and the side of the face.

The drawing must never be taken for gospel during the painting, but merely as a rough guide. When it comes to overlaying the oil paint, constant modifications will be necessary. And this means checking for accuracy.

Once I was happy with the pencil drawing, I overlaid the lines with thinned blue acrylic paint via a fine sable. This will ensure the lines will remain visible beneath the underglaze, which will be applied once the blue paint has dried.

Purpose of the Underglaze

In order to kill the whiteness of the art surface, a thin glaze will be applied over the drawing. This will kill the white art surface and enable the artist to judge tonal values more accurately

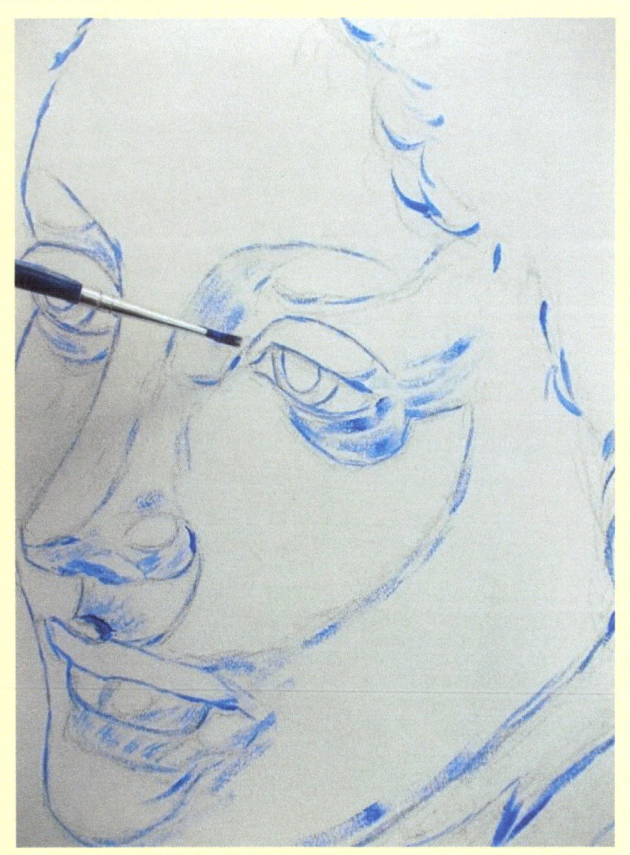

As has been discussed, painting straight onto a white art surface can be off-putting. To remedy this, diluted oil paint can be used, but I prefer acrylic paint diluted with water. Any colour can be used to inject mood into the overlying paint. Here, I used a warm colour.

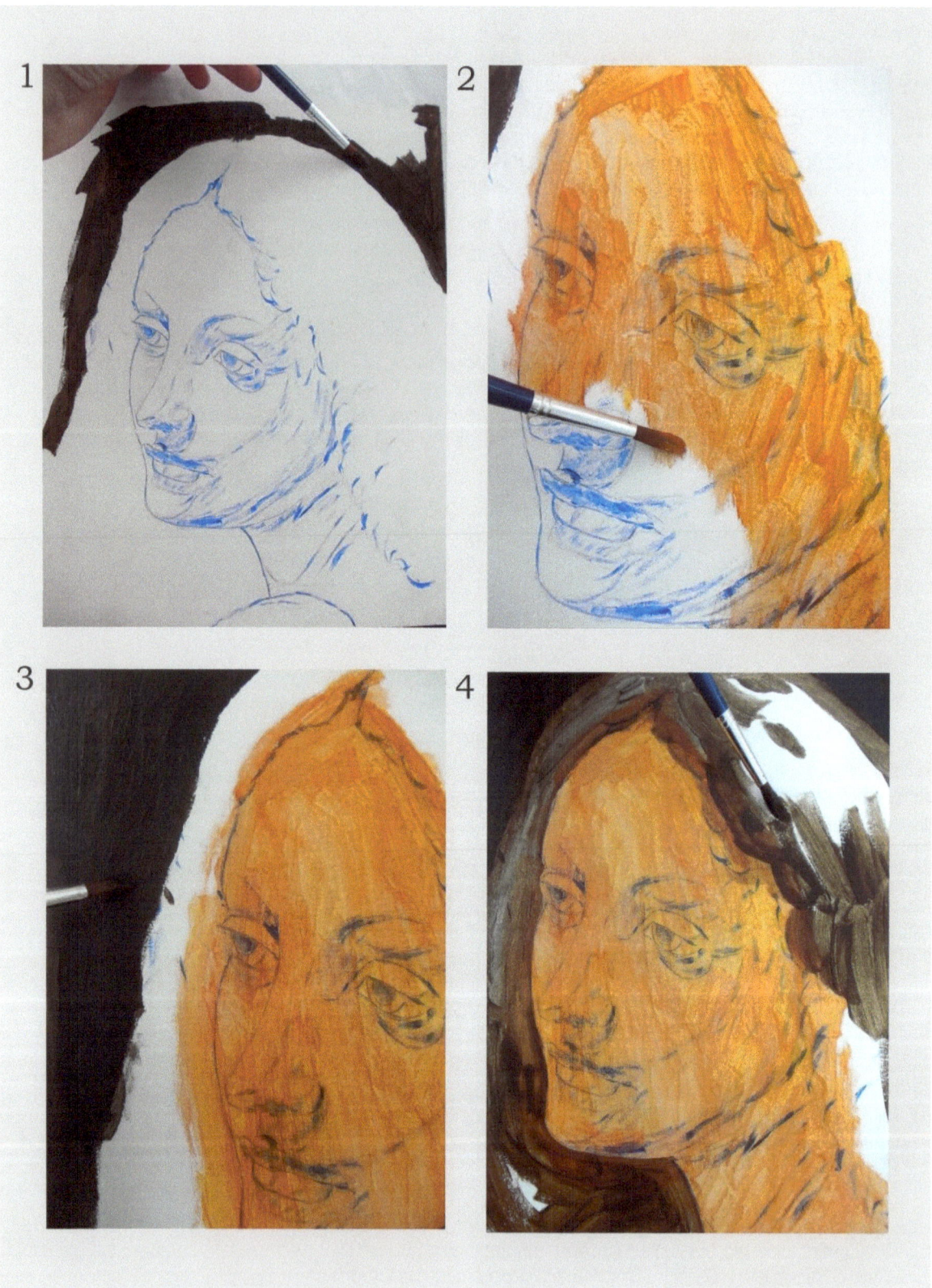

Applying the Underglaze

1 The project has already begun, as previously described via the reinforcement of lines from diluted blue acrylic paint. The sketch will remain visible beneath the underglaze about to be applied, as blue and orange are opposing colours. However, for the background, I will use a solid colour.

Firstly with a wide sable, I blocked in the background around the head with neat burnt umber acrylic paint. Applying the dark background this early in the painting provides a benchmark from which to judge highlights and mid-tones of the face.

Leaving the background white will make skin colours, however pale, appear darker than they really are. This could result in a washed-out looking portrait painting that will require unnecessary fiddling over to put things right.

Keying in Tones

2 Once the background colour was dry, I applied a dilute acrylic orange-brown mix via a medium sable over the face. I mixed a small blob each of alizarin crimson with cadmium yellow into a pot containing a few drops of water. I kept mixing until all the paint had dissolved into the water.

A perfectly smooth glaze is not the aim, but to simply inject a warm undercurrent into the skin tones. Don't worry if these pigments are not available. Any warm colour will do, including cadmium orange, cadmium red or burnt sienna. Ensure the tint is not too thin or diluted, but permits the underdrawing to show through.

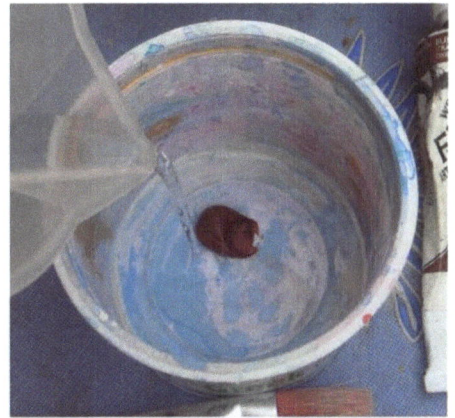

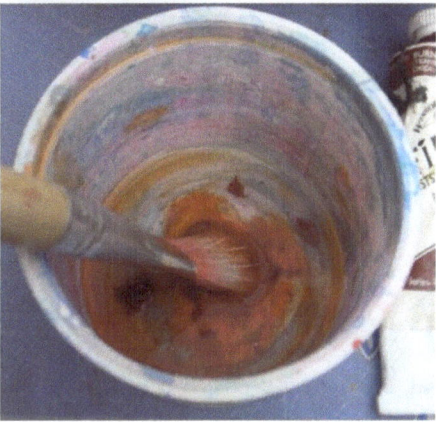

A blob of orange-brown acrylic paint diluted with a few drops of water to make it flow before applying the underglaze.

3 By now, the burnt umber applied onto the background was dry. However, even the most opaque paint will appear uneven on close inspection, which makes a second coat often necessary. With a medium bristle, I applied a second layer of burnt umber acrylic paint over the background once the first coat was dry.

With a slightly thinner mix of burnt umber, I went over the hair, bringing the paint up to the edges of the face. This thinner mix differentiates between the opaque background colour and of the hair area.

Acrylic's quick drying time without the need for solvents makes the acrylic glaze more convenient to use than the traditional thinned oil paint. Depending upon the atmospheric conditions, the acrylic glaze will dry between 1 to 2 hours.

4 Once the orange glaze applied over the face earlier had dried, I applied a second glaze to deepen the tone a little more and to even out the wash. My pot of dilute acrylic mix was still usable. With a, soft bristle I applied the glaze over the face. Once the acrylic glaze was dry, the oil paint can be applied on top.

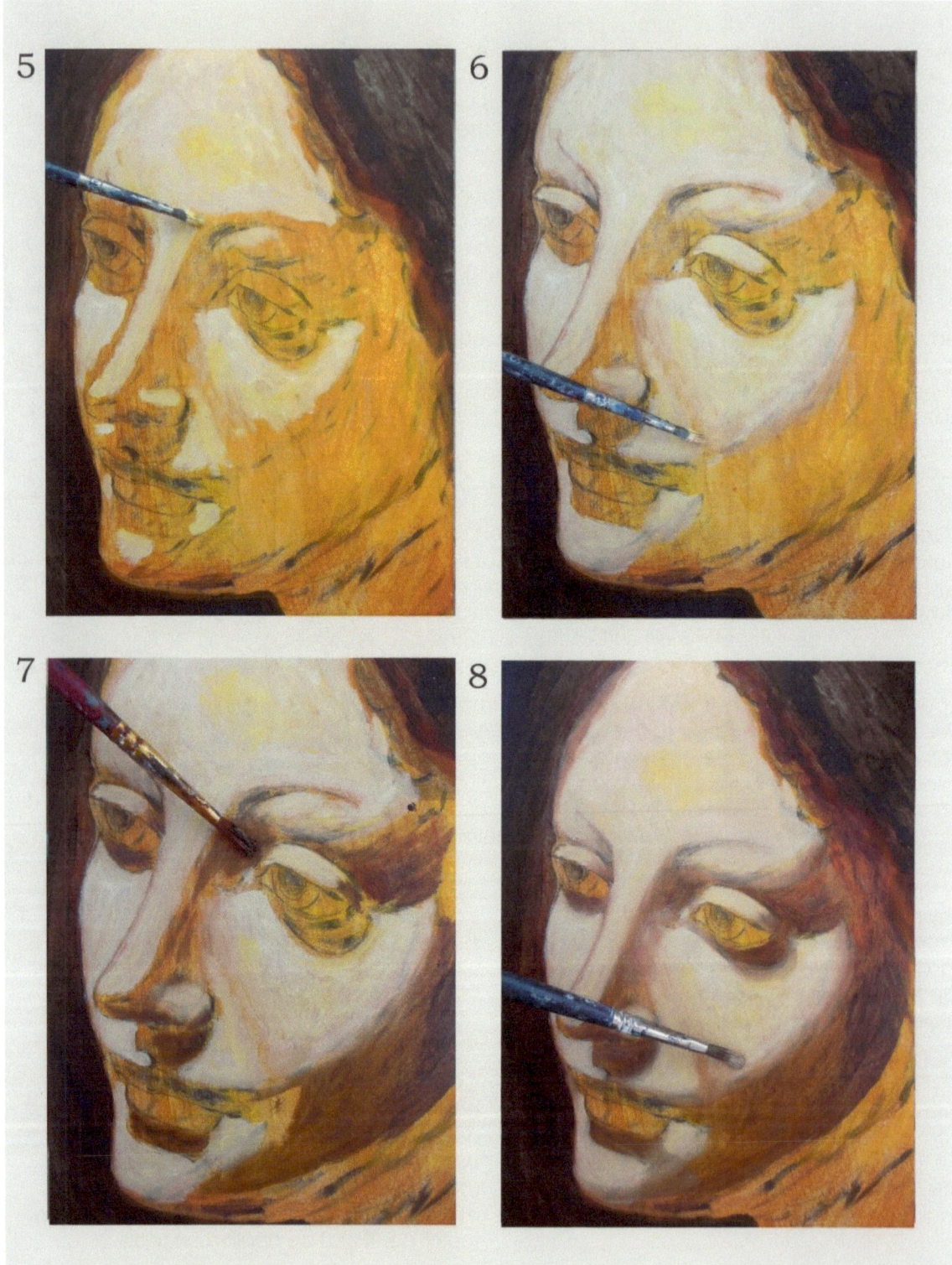

The First Mark

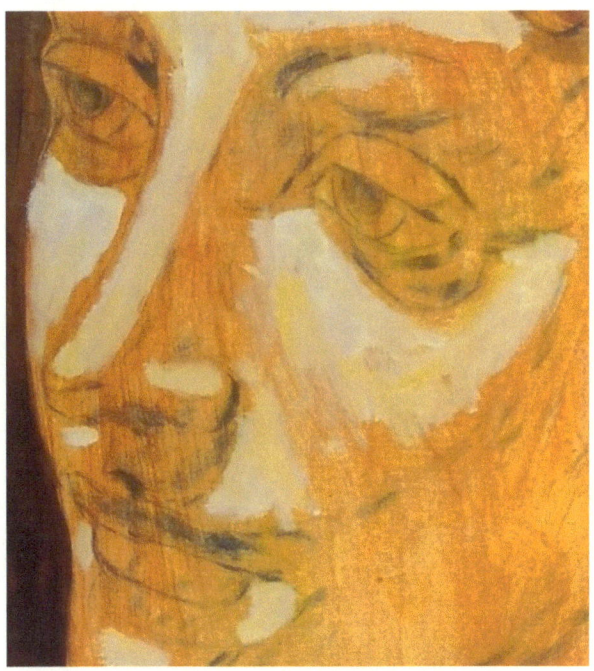

This first glaze of oil paint will provide the foundation onto which *sfumato* and smooth effects can be built, which makes it a crucial element.

5 It is advisable to begin this chief stage on a separate day to the preliminary stages when feeling up to the challenge. With a medium sable, I mixed mostly white with a little cadmium yellow and burnt sienna to achieve a pale marzipan hue.

The pigment was spread thinly across the cheekbones, ridge of the nose and across the brow. I viewed the highlights of the face as abstract shapes of light.

Notice how the colour is spread more thinly towards the edges where they will melt into shadow. Care is needed to reflect the complex colour shapes around the nose ad chin.

Edges of Highlight

6 With the same sable, I worked the paint towards the edges of highlights without adding more pigment to the brush. Notice the various ways in which light melts into shadow upon the angel's face. In some areas, the transition is gradual; in others, it appears more abrupt.

For the sotter edges, I added a lillle burnt sienna to the cream colour mix and softened the edge of highlight to the temple, cheek and chin. The resultant increment in tone suggests the shifting contours of the face.

7 With a separate sable reserved for dark colours, I mixed a little burnt umber into burnt sienna and sketched in the shadows, working from the darkest areas of the face. This included the inner eye sockets, above the eyelids, lower jaw, beneath the nose and the chin. Notice how the shadow softens and breaks up midway along the side of the nose. A thinner paint mix was applied here.

These rudimentary patches of pale and dark colour can be viewed as a jigsaw that comes together to suggest a face. The features suddenly become clear, particularly how one relates with another. It is never too late to make modifications to these colour shapes if an issue jumps out at you. This might be an overlooked patch of light or a shadow of the wrong shape. Standing back from the painting will afford an overall view of this jigsaw. Only once reasonably accuracy of these shapes has been achieved will I begin the next stage.

8 With a clean medium sable, I closed the seams between pale and dark colours. For the cheekbone, temple and side of the nose, I pulled the dark colour into the pales and created a soft blend where the two meet. In order to retain control, I periodically wiped excess paint onto a rag and continued to blend.

Remember not to blend colour seams in the same manner throughout the painting. Steep tonal gradations, as seen around the nub of the nose, shadow over the philtrum (the area between the nose and mouth) and the eyelids need to be retained. However, a few strokes of the brush are required in order to conceal the acrylic underglaze beneath.

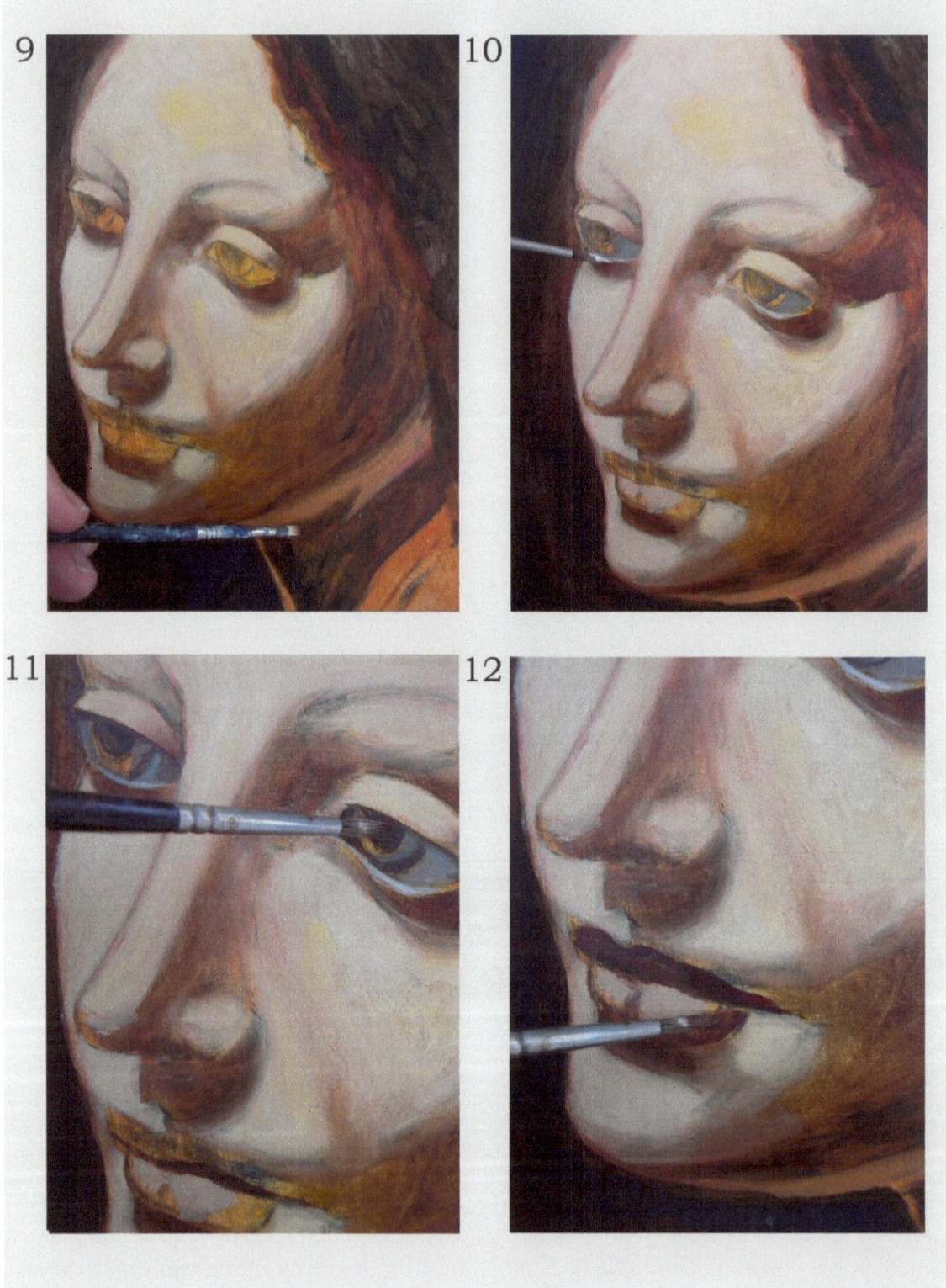

Opposing Sources of Light

9 the reflected light beneath the jaw is subtle but vital in that it describes the underside of the face. The colour is not the same as highlight but lies someway between light and dark. With the 'pale' sable used in step 5, I mixed burnt sienna, burnt umber, cadmium yellow and a little white. This warm colour was then applied just above the neckline.

10 With a fine sable, I mixed white with a little burnt sienna and tracked a fine line along the lower eye rims. Soften harsh division between this line and the adjacent shadows beneath that could look harsh and synthetic.

Notice how the highlight varies along the way, giving into shadow towards the sides of the face. With the same brush, I softened tonal division around the eyelids.

I added a little white with burnt sienna and pthalo blue and then worked this colour around the eyeballs. Overrule the knowledge that eyeballs are generally white and

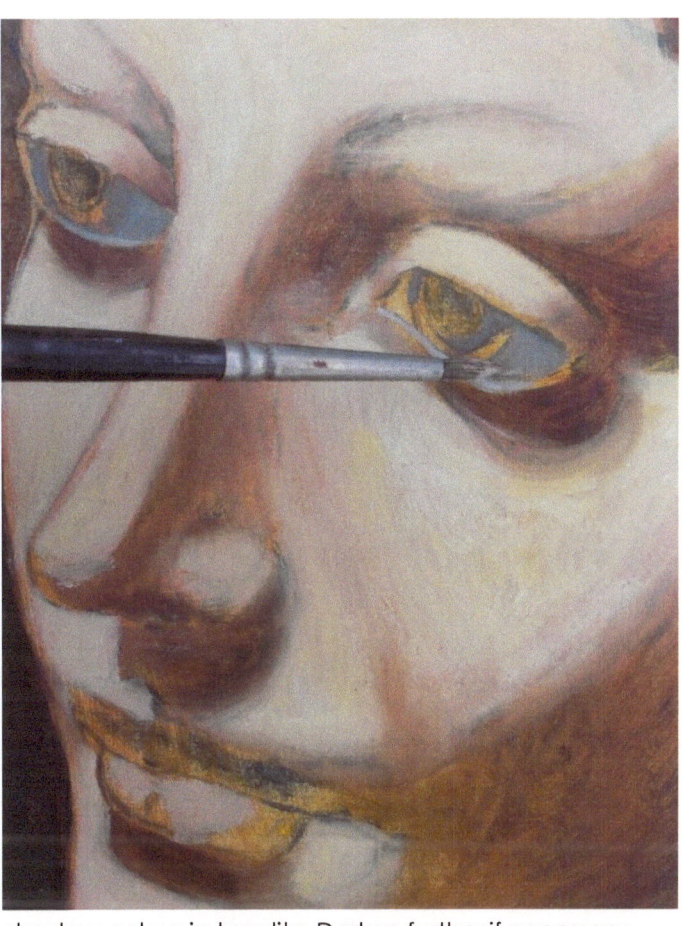

aim for a grayish-blue that matches the shadow colour in tonality. Darken further if necessary.

11 With the same sable, I added more pthalo blue and a little of this cream colour and applied this bluish-grey mix onto the irises. A dark delineation around the iris was suggested via a fifty-fifty mix of pthalo blue and burnt umber. This dark colour was also blended out from beneath the eyelids to suggest shadow.

Finally, I cleaned the brush and mixed an almost black colour of burnt umber and pthalo blue. Both pupils were illustrated. Check for: **a**) their sizes are similar; **b**) their direction of gaze is consistent and **c**) how much is visible beneath the eyelids.

This part is important, so take the time to get it right. Amendments can be made by gently wiping off the erroneous paint and reapplying.

When Lips are Not Red

12 As can be seen here, the angel's lips are luscious but far from red, in fact, darks far outweigh any colour.

With a clean sable, I dabbed white with a little alizarin crimson and pthalo blue onto the lower lip. Notice a band of shadow splitting the highlight into two. With the same sable, I added a little more alizarin crimson, pthalo blue and burnt umber before applying it onto the upper lip.

As can be seen here, the violet-brown colour is uniform. I wiped excess paint from the brush and blended the lip colour slightly into the adjacent skin shadows to the sides of the mouth to eradicate harsh lines.

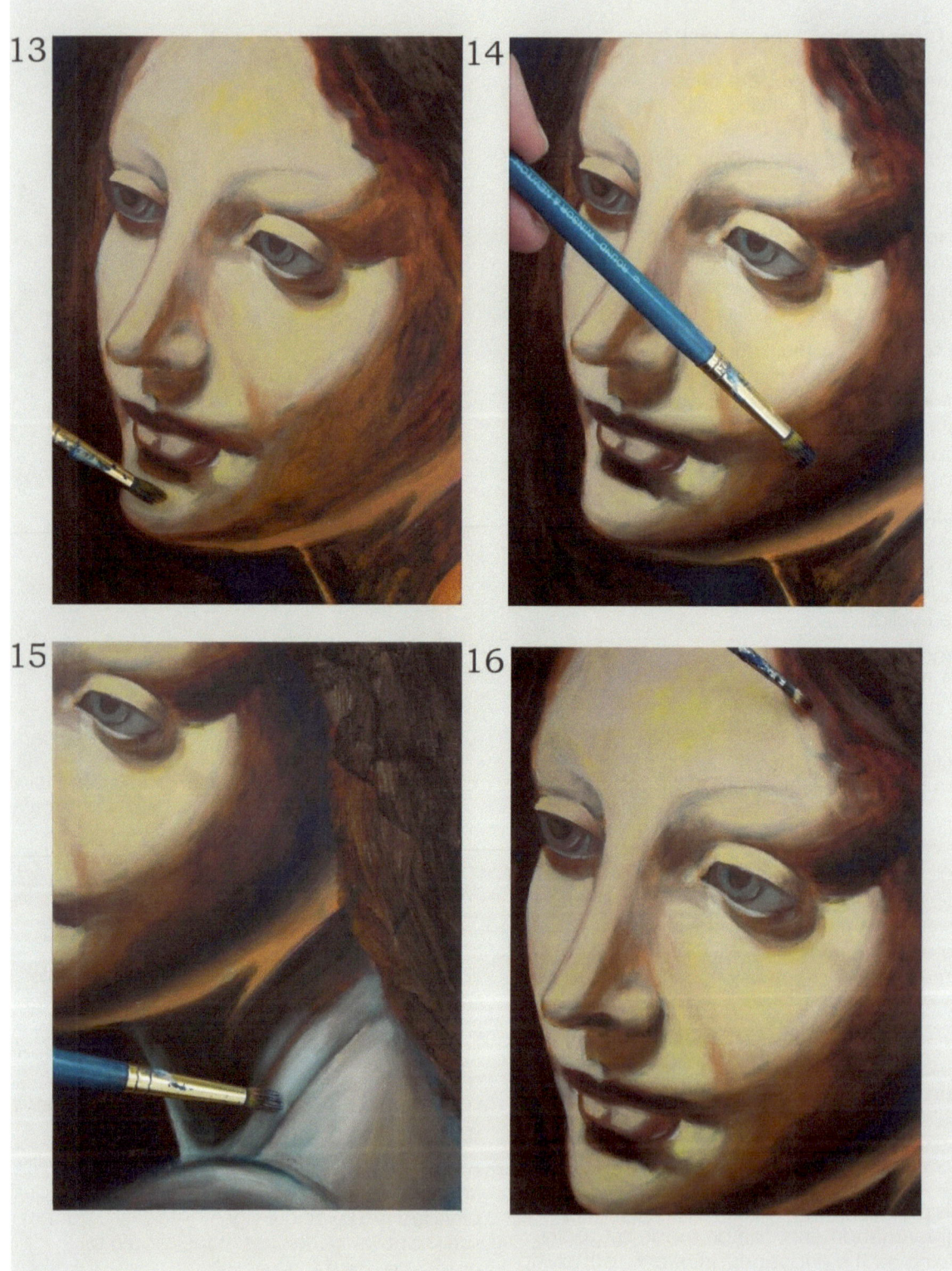

Smoothing the First Glaze

13 With the first oil glaze now covering the entire face area, the artist can make further modifications to the painting as the oil slowly dries. By this point, I had been working for about an hour. The oil paint on the palette had thickened slightly in the air, particularly the faster-drying burnt umber. Such a consistency is ideal for perfecting blends, providing the foundation for *sfumato* effects to be applied at a later stage. With a clean sable, I went over the pale areas again, adding a little more pigment to areas revealing the acrylic underglaze and smoothing out brush marks. Don't overload the brush or work too vigorously or this could ruin the smooth effects so far applied.

14 I practiced the same method with the dark areas with a separate sable. I dabbed a little burnt sienna onto the ends of the bristles and gently applied strokes to the broad expanses of the cheek working from the temple to the chin. A little additional pthalo blue and burnt umber may be needed to reinforce the smooth tonal gradation to the dark band of shadow on the lower cheek. Be careful not to let the endeavour

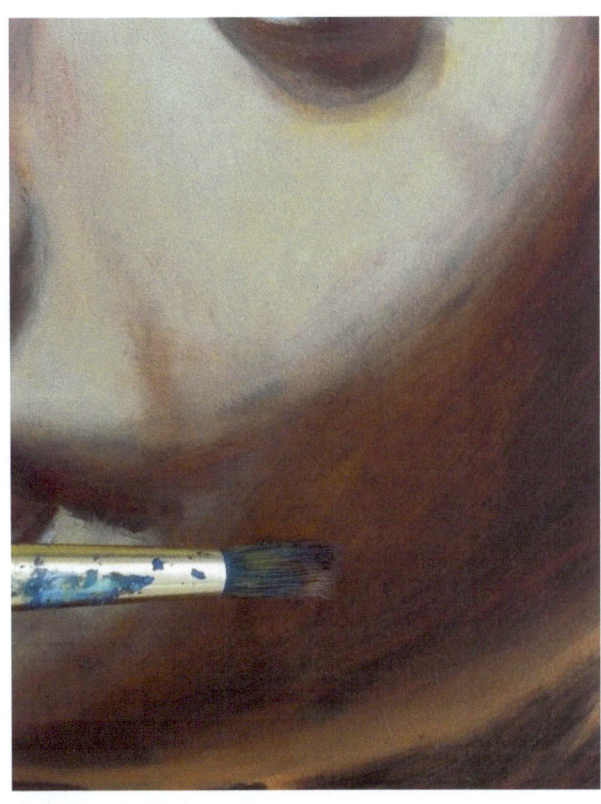

to smooth blends to obscure the maintenance of accuracy. A beautifully blended shadow is not good if it is of the wrong shape or tonal value. This might allow the left brain to fill in gaps for an artist who becomes preoccupied with one aspect of the painting. Remember to keep looking and to stand back from the painting to gain an overall view of the colour shapes.

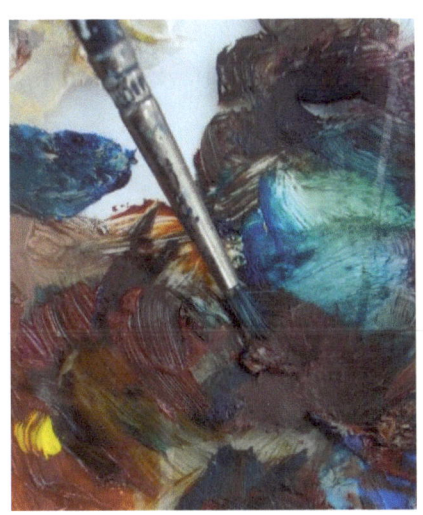

Warm and Cool Skin Tones

15 The neck, having a cool colour cast to the face, can be painted on a separate day. But uphold the earlier principle of treating each glaze as though to be the last, in spite of the scope for future modifications. Only then did I embark upon the neck, which possesses cool colours. With a medium bristle, I applied the shadow colour first, which matches that of the background. Neat burnt umber was worked across the underside of the jaw.

With a separate bristle, I applied white with a little pthalo blue and burnt umber to express the cool highlights. A fine bristle was used to delineate the folds in the neck. These are not mere lines but soft ridges. A progressively darker hue suggests these undulations.

16 With the same bristle I added burnt sienna, a little cadmium yellow and white and then blended out the shadow between brow and the hairline. This will provide the foundation onto which to express detail. Keep working across the hair boundary to soften transitions in tone.

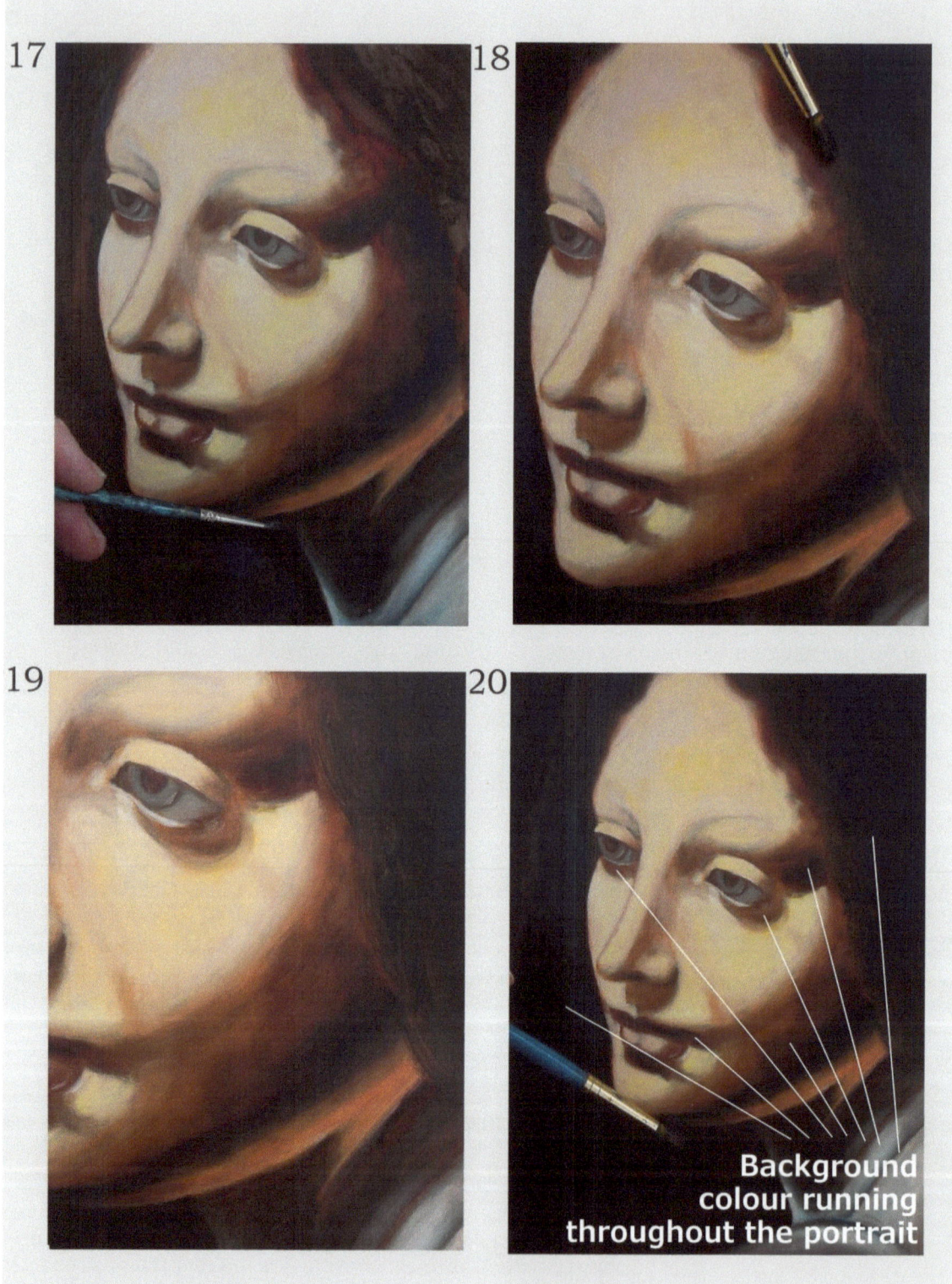

Background
colour running
throughout the portrait

Background Colour within the Figure

17 All tonal values have been used in this initial oil glaze from very pale to almost black. Such judgments of tone would have been difficult had it not been for the dark brown background previously applied. Having served its purpose, an oil glaze can now be applied on top to provide accordance with the shadows on the face.

With a wide bristle, I spread burnt umber oil paint throughout the background, adding a little burnt sienna at the top to suggest a light source. A fine bristle was used for tricky outlines such as the chin. Aim for an even paint layer with minimal brush marks to create the ideal foundation on which to practice *sfumato*.

18 this final stage of the foundation glaze is vital before putting the painting away, for It provides the last say regarding how the shadow colours of the background run throughout the subject matter. This will help make the angel appear to 'belong' to the space she resides, as opposed to being cut out and glued onto a background that doesn't quite match. The four images possessing different-coloured backgrounds illustrate this point.

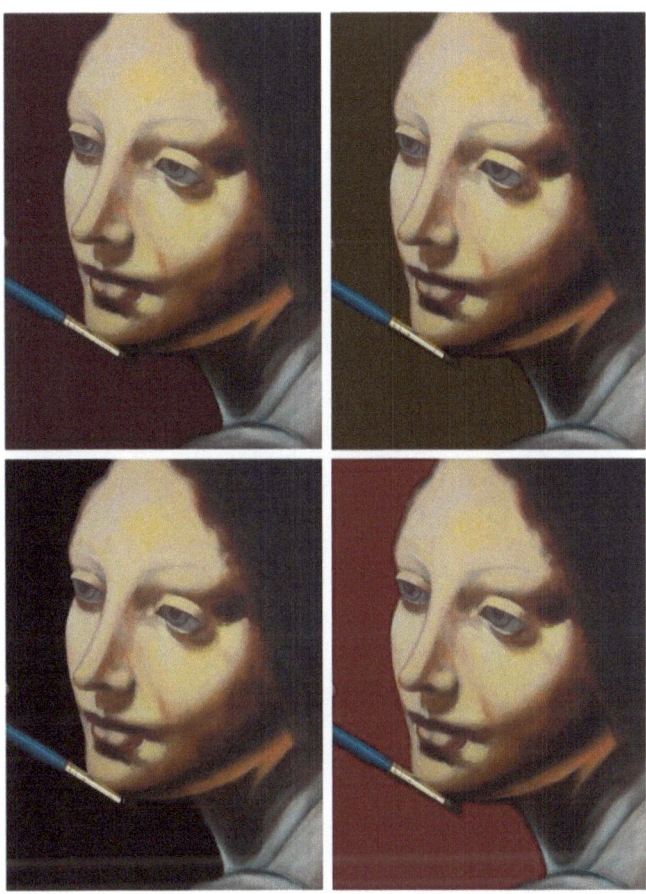

Correct any colour casts that do not quite match the shadows on the face, whether it is slightly too green, yellow, maroon or simply too dark. The aim is to make the angel appear to emerge from the shadows. This is vital for effective *sfumato* effects to be perfected later.

19 With a medium bristle, I dabbed burnt umber oil paint onto the darkest portions of the face, smoothing out any areas that contain brush marks. This is especially important on the broad expanses of the face, such as the cheek and brow.

Before finishing the first glaze, stand back and look for any tonal imbalances. Does any highlight fail to describe form and appear flat? This may occur on the brow, cheekbone or beneath the eyes. Is any shadow too dark, creating an unwanted focal point? This may occur on the shadow beneath the nose or on the temple.

An Overall View

20 Finally, a medium sable was used to dab the darkest shadow colour into portions of the face, including the lower jaw, temple and chin. The effect aimed for is that the background appears to 'leach' in into sections of the face, becoming part of her.

Sfumato is all about light and shadow running throughout the entire painting in a similar fashion.

Ensure the highlights and shadows fit together in the manner reflected in Da Vinci's painting. Make amendments whilst the oil paint is still workable. Blending will no longer be possible on the next session.

27

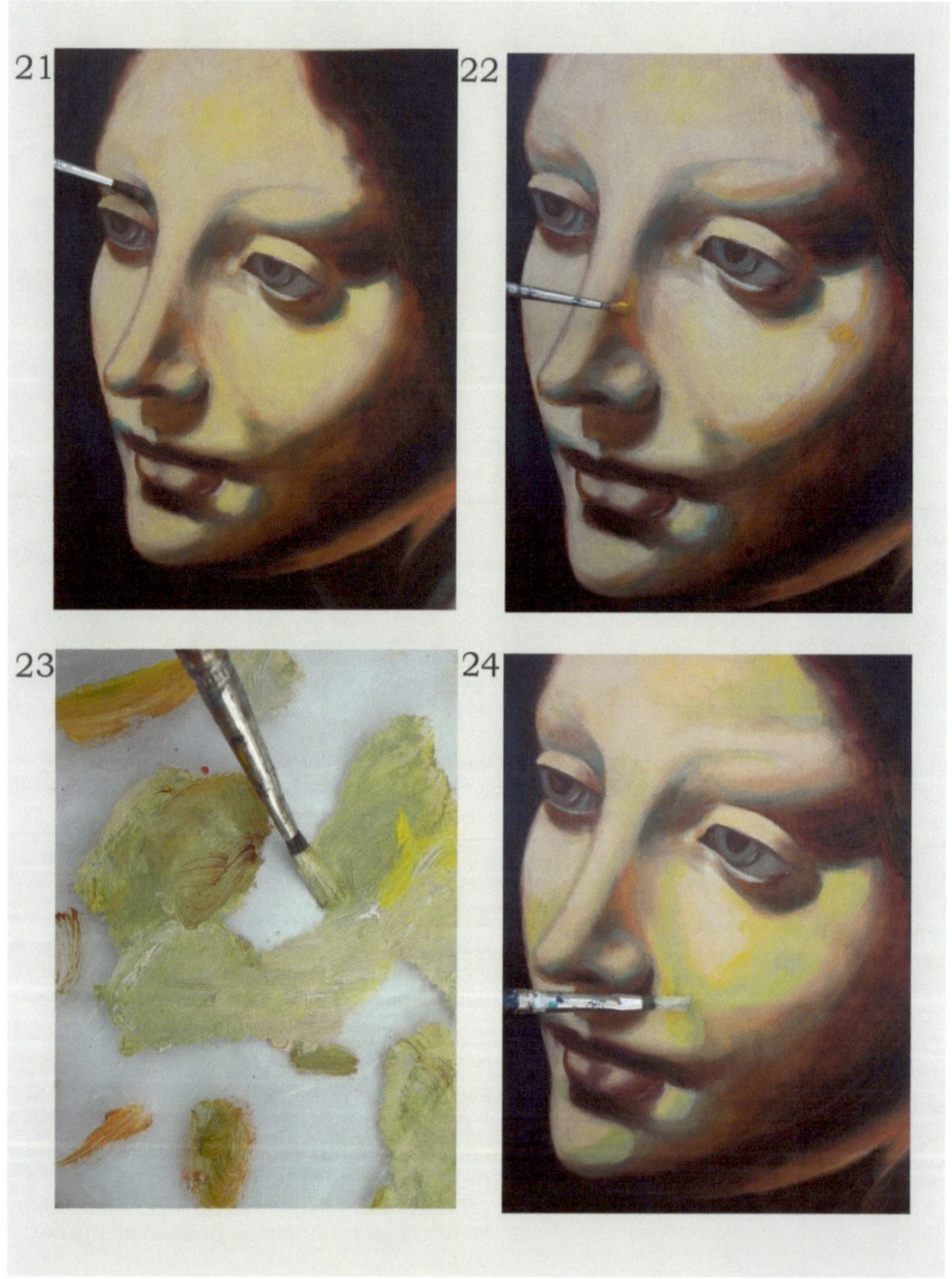

Sunset Colours

THIS SECOND oil glaze requires a little courage due to the bands of colour that can be discerned on the angel's face where light and shadow meet. This, as well as the *sfumato* effects, creates great challenges for the portraitist.

After two days, the foundation glaze had become touch-dry, meaning the oil paint is no longer workable. But applying the next glaze will create greater depth of colour and tone.

Having not seen *the Virgin of the Rocks* in the flesh, cannot be certain of how faithful the reproduction is, but all have a colour bias, no matter how accurate the print may be. This one provided great interest, as gold, crimson, blue and even green can be seen at the junction of light and shadow. This I felt provided an extra element to the customary tobacco hues associated with *sfumato*.

21 A degree of bravery is required here, as applying green to a face would go against the orthodox notion of the colours seen within a portrait. With a fine bristle, I made preliminary dabs of viridian, softened with white, cadmium yellow and burnt sienna. Select areas were elaborated upon, chiefly, the upper outlines of shadows. I expressed a greenish cast around the upper brow-bone of the eye socket, the ridge of the nose, the nub and the chin. The stiff bristle enabled me to apply this definite hue quite thinly. If it appears too heavy, wipe off the excess with a clean bristle or a rag.

22 With a separate fine bristle, I applied a little alizarin crimson with burnt sienna and white and dabbed this warm colour adjacent to the green, which included the midpoint of the nose's flank, above the eyelids and temple. Be careful not to let the two colours contaminate one another or a muddy mix could result, as both are complementary to one another. Smudge out the edges with a clean bristle to attain soft effects.

Tinted Neutrals

23 This view of the mixing palette shows how the green colour used in step 21 had been muted by the addition of burnt sienna, cadmium yellow and white. As can be seen, large amounts of perfectly-mixed pigment is not required. In fact, variations are preferable. In isolation, the colour mix can appear quite muted and grey, but has a greenish appearance once applied onto the skin colour.

24 This soft, yellowy-green colour was applied around the fringes of highlight, including the outer contours of the cheek, side of the nose and beneath the mouth. Additional white and burnt sienna was added to blend this sage colour into highlight.

This glaze is applied progressively thinly towards the adjacent cream colours of the cheekbones in order to retain the feeling of a light effect as opposed to the actual colour of the cheekbones.

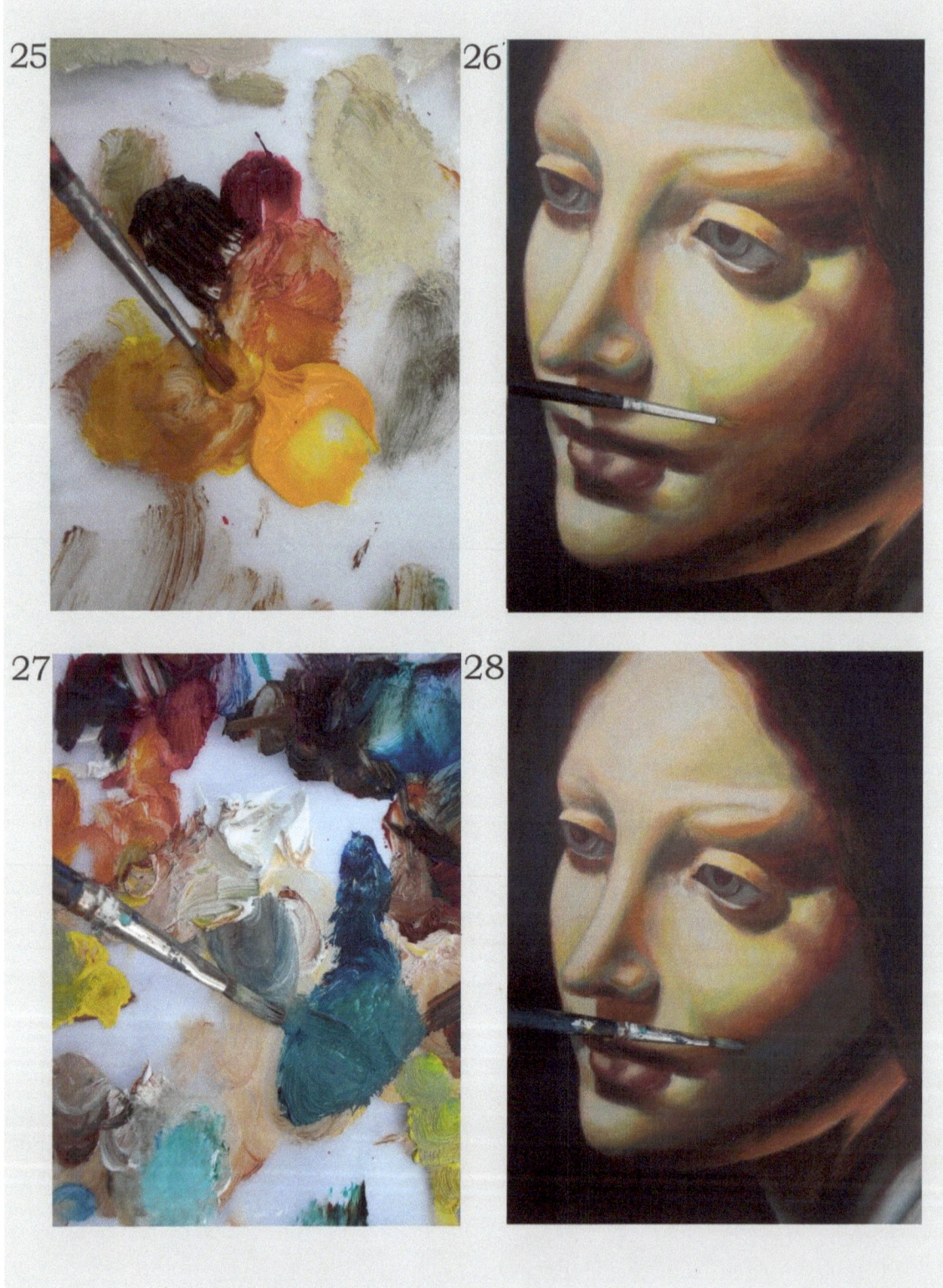

A Soft Shift in Hue

25 The second band of colour was elaborated upon. Here, the mixing palette displays the blending of alizarin crimson, burnt sienna, cadmium yellow and a little white. Again, notice the variations in hue as it is applied. In some places, it has a honey hue, in others, it appears gold, or russet. This organic approach reflects the subject matter.

26 Just a small amount of this rich gold colour is needed to bring out the warmth to the shadows. I ran the bristle down the cheekbone, above the eye sockets, temple and towards the chin. A little was also applied to the reflected light to add richness.

I wiped excess paint from the bristle until almost none remained and smudged the pigment into the highlights. Being heavy-handed is a constant danger here, as colours become more significant with every glaze. Stand back to ensure the skin tones do not appear overly flushed or too green. With a clean, soft bristle, I pulled the more powerful russets into the delicate pale greens, to attain sunset colours. Take care that the two colours do not mix too much. A soft division between the two is the aim.

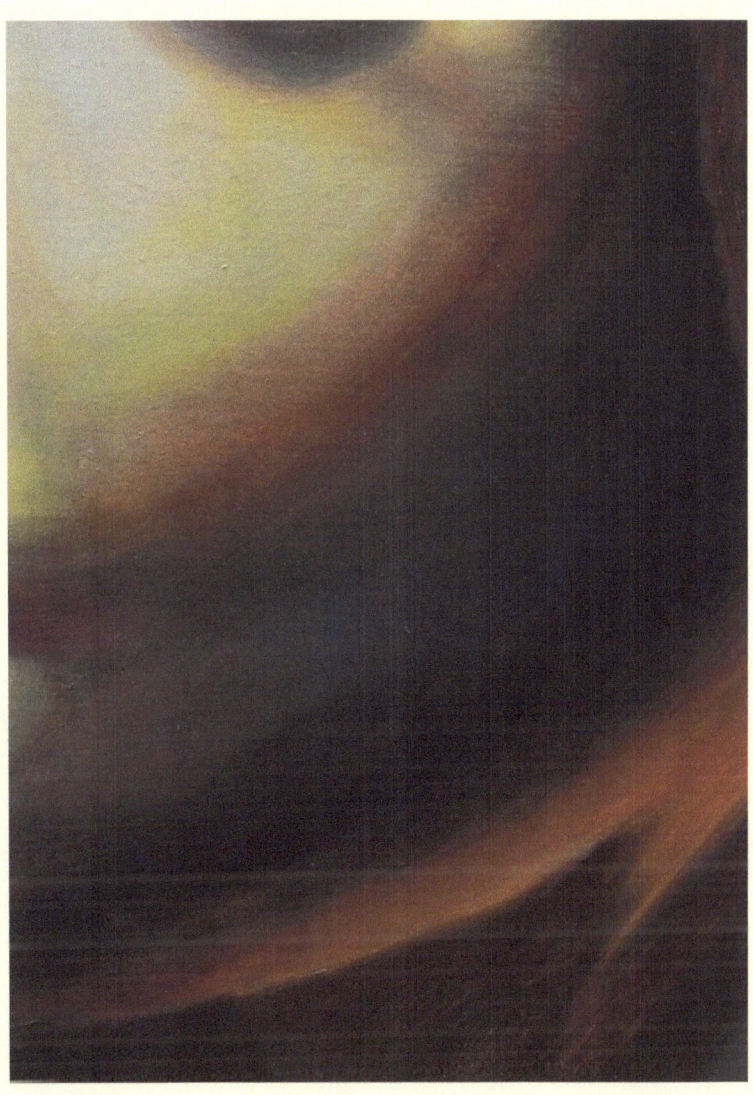

27 And now for the final band of colour. Here, we can see the mixing palette of pthalo blue, burnt sienna, a little alizarin crimson and white. An almost neutral colour is the aim, but one that is biased towards blue – a soft, smoky kind.

Getting the right tonal balance will require a few test dabs of paint just below the russet band. The colour temperature should be cooler, but of a similar tone to the red, as can be seen in the next step's image.

Fine-Tuning Blends

28 This smoky blue colour was thinly applied over the lower cheek, lightly smudging into the main body of shadow. A little additional burnt umber was added to provide a smooth transition between soft blue and dark brown.

Take care not to get carried away with blending, as the bands of colour could get muddied. With a little additional white, a slightly paler blue was dabbed onto select areas of the nub of the nose, chin and above the eye sockets. This brings the rest of the face into accordance.

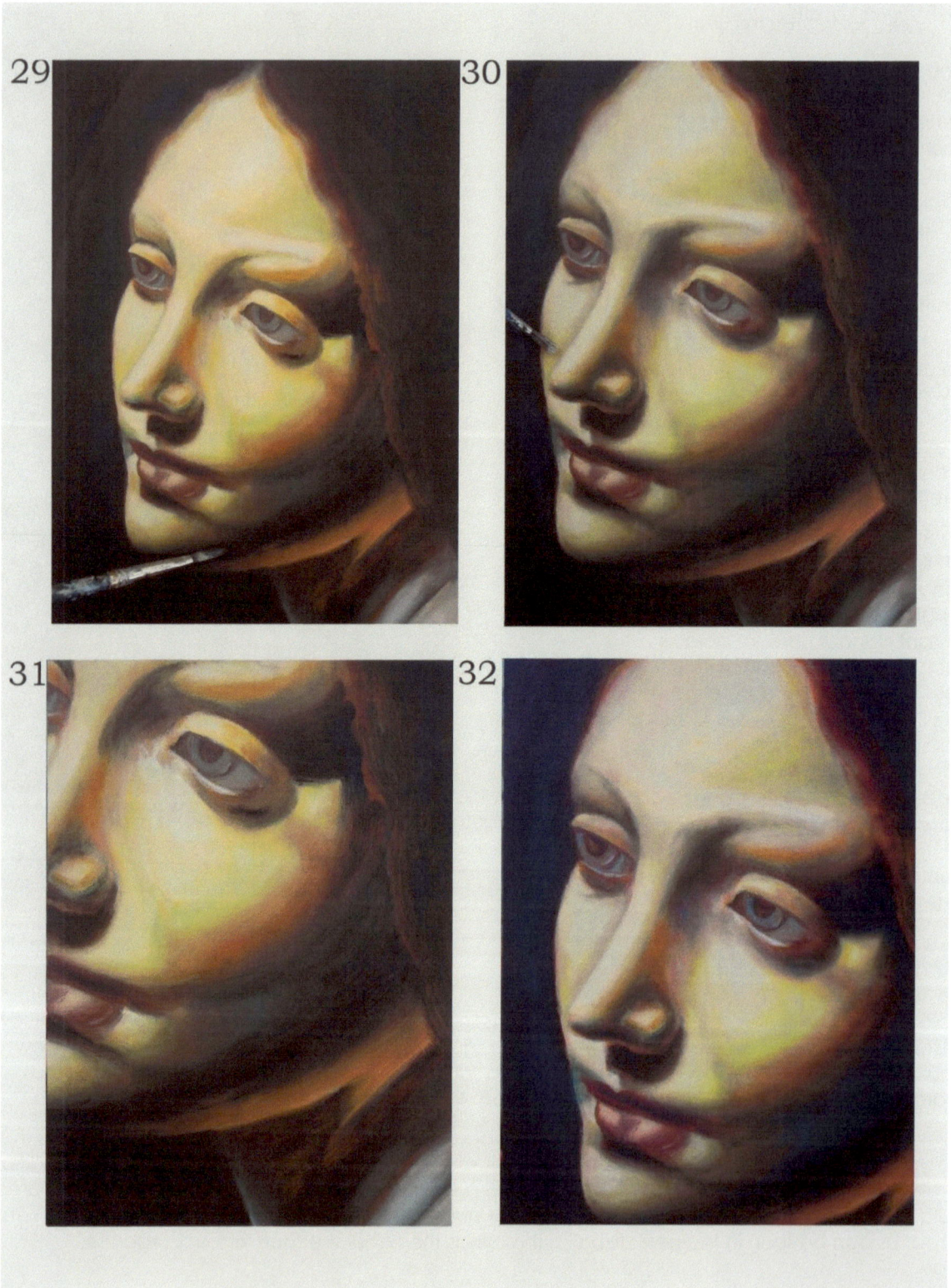

The Shape of Reflected Light

29 I wiped excess paint from the brush and carefully smudged one band of colour into another as necessary. The sole aim is to eradicate steep shifts in hue. But also one which allows the bands of colour to remain. With a medium sable, I reinforced the darkest bands of shadow via burnt umber and pthalo blue. A little white might be necessary if the colour is too heavy. These darkest bands were expressed just above the jaw line, taking care not to contaminate the area of reflected light adjacent.

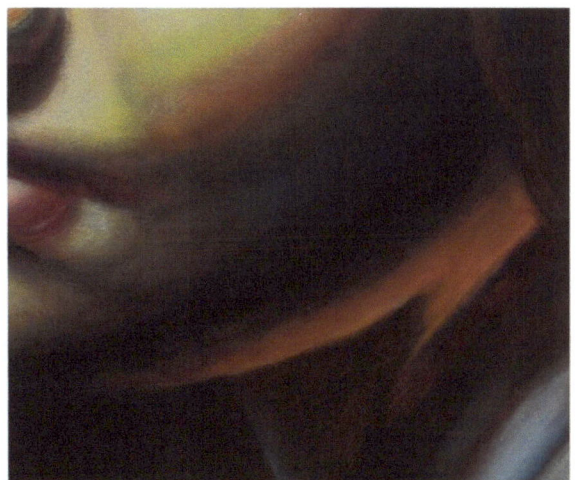

I wiped excess paint from the brush and softened the upper edge of the reflected light. Notice how the outline of this shape varies. The upper edge is soft; the lower edge is more defined. Retaining these differences will help describe form, as can be seen in the images during the blending process.

30 The highlights of the face were touched up via a clean sable by the application of white and a little burnt sienna. A thin glaze was applied to the upper cheekbones, brow and protrusion on the chin. I wiped excess paint from the brush and pulled the adjacent greenish tinge upwards to create a very soft gradation. Notice how this shift in hue is more gradual on broad planes of the face such as the cheekbones, but is less so around the nose, mouth and eye sockets. But regardless of how steep the gradation, all colour shifts must be soft.

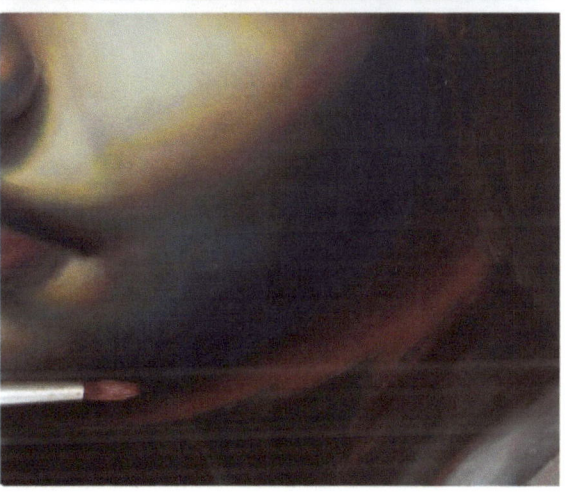

While the Paint is Workable

31 This close-up image shows the bands of colour at the junction of light and shadow. It begins with creamy highlights shifting to sage green, a deep green (in places), gold, russet, smoky blue and then dark brown.

No two bands must produce a dirty band of colour, but lead into each other via a progressively thinner glaze. Continue to work over the painting with a soft bristle, holding almost no pigment. Keep softening the shadows whilst the paint is workable

32 As always, stand back from the painting and make necessary modification before putting it away to dry for the next glaze.

Treating every glaze as though to be the last means each paint layer will support the next.

So ensure the following before allowing the painting to dry: **A)** That the shadow colour of the portrait roughly reflects that of the background to help support *sfumato*. **B)** That there are no rough blends on the face that could draw the eye.

And **C)** That no shadow has been overlooked. This includes the faint band of shadow that joins the lower left eyelid to the temple; the triangular shadow on the right side of the mouth; the faint ridge of shadow above the left eyebrow, and a faint trough of shadow between the nose and mouth.

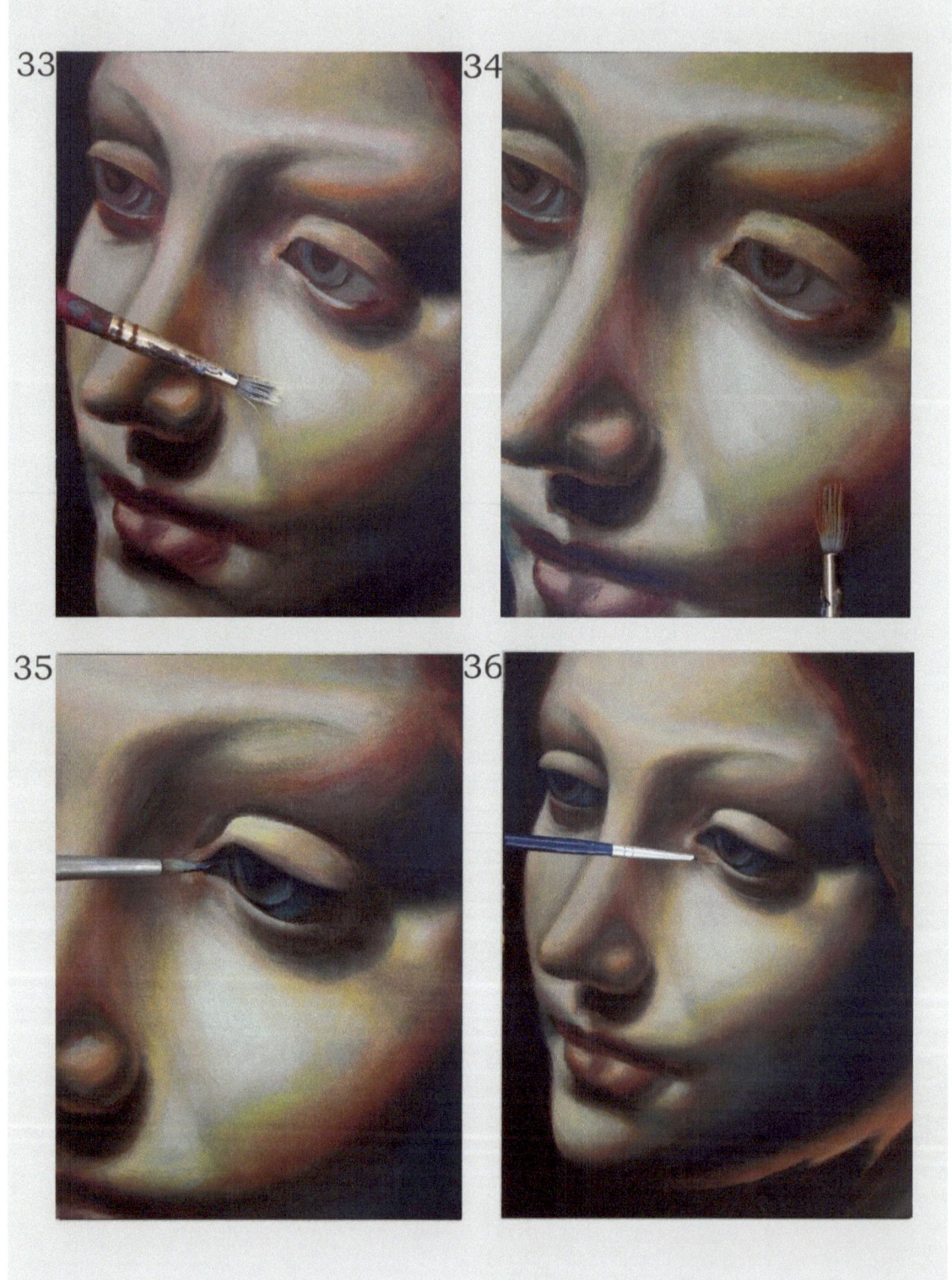

A Fine Dusting of Paint

A FINE GLAZE of oil paint once dry will appear a little less refined than when the paint was workable. Blends may not appear so smooth and imperfections may become more obvious. Don't worry, as this is the nature of glazing technique. Each layer will work with the previous glaze to attain a higher finish. Observe how each glaze requires a little less work than the last, as the foundations have already been laid. This penultimate glaze required an hour or so.

33 Once the oil paint was touch-dry after two days or so, I refined smooth blends where necessary. A soft sable bearing a little white and burnt sienna was gently dabbed over the cheek, bridge across the brow, highlights on either side of the philtrum and the chin. Observe the added significance of each brush mark compared to the earlier glazes.

34 A fine dusting of burnt sienna was applied onto the russet band of colour across the cheek, temple, above the eye sockets and side of the nose. The image shows the small amount of pigment required to make a difference.

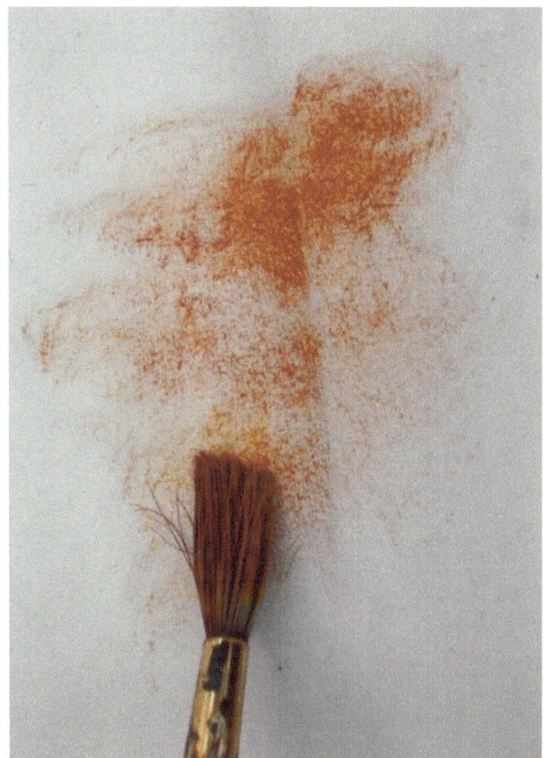

Other artists may feel the need to employ this treatment for a different band of colour, which might be green or blue. Notice the greater depth of tone and richness to the hues. I used the colour more sparingly as I worked into shadow, ensuring smooth blends are retained.

The Colour of the Eyeball

35 To this point, I had applied mere rudimentary colours to the eyes, with the sole aim of concealing the underglaze. Applying high detail to the eyes early in the painting will result in a dominant focal point before issues with the surrounding skin colour have been resolved. For this reason, I will often work detail into the eyes in the closing stages of the painting.

With a fine sable, I mixed pthalo blue, burnt umber and a little white. This steely grey colour is not for the irises but the eyeballs. Under certain lighting conditions the eyeballs can appear darker than the surrounding skin. I dabbed this dark colour onto the area concerned.

With the same sable, I darkened the colour with pthalo blue and adjusted the size of both pupils until they were of the same size and looking the same way. Notice they occupy a large portion of the irises, adding a dreamy aspect to her gaze.

With the same colour, I added definition to the outlines of the irises.

36 Whilst in the eye area, I fine-tuned mini shadows around the rims of the eyes and the lower eyelids. A little pthalo blue, burnt umber and white was applied via a clean sable beneath the eyes.

A fleck of burnt sienna, alizarin crimson with a little white was dabbed around the tear duct and the side of the nose for warmer hues. The outline of eye rims and the eyelids were finally softened into the surrounding skin colour. With additional white and cadmium yellow, I blended the transition between light and shadow over the eyelids.

Deliberating over the skin surrounding the eyes is key to painting effective eyes, as they set the stage for the subject's gaze. As can be seen here, the eyes are more than just about the pupils and the colour of the irises.

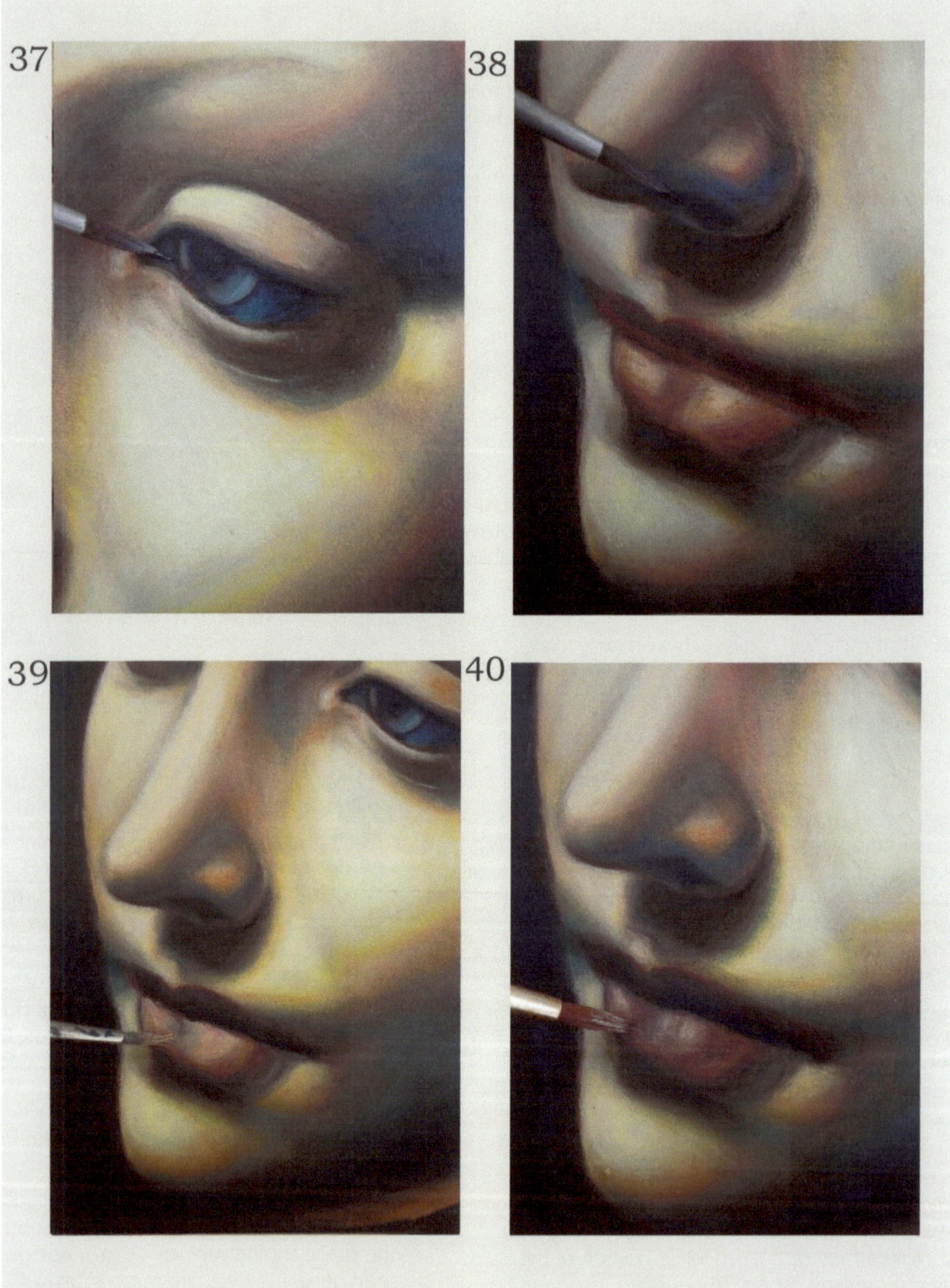

Detail within the Eyes

37 With a little pthalo blue and white, I pulled the shadow colour beneath the eyelids into the main colour of the eyeballs. This creates the impression of overhanging shadow and suggests the spherical shape of the eyeballs.

Additional white was used to reinforce soft highlights on the eyeballs. With the same colour, I dabbed faint crescent-shaped highlights on the irises to bring out the translucence of the angel's eyes.

38 With the 'dark' sable used in step 35, I elaborated upon the nub and the base of the nose. The left nostril is only just visible within shadow but provides vital visual information on the portrait.

Notice the shape is elliptical but squashed on one side. I carefully made preliminary marks before going over it with deeper colours. I softened outlines between this dark colour and the surrounding shadow colour to prevent a 'cutout' look to the nostril.

With the same colour mix, I added definition to the base of the nose.

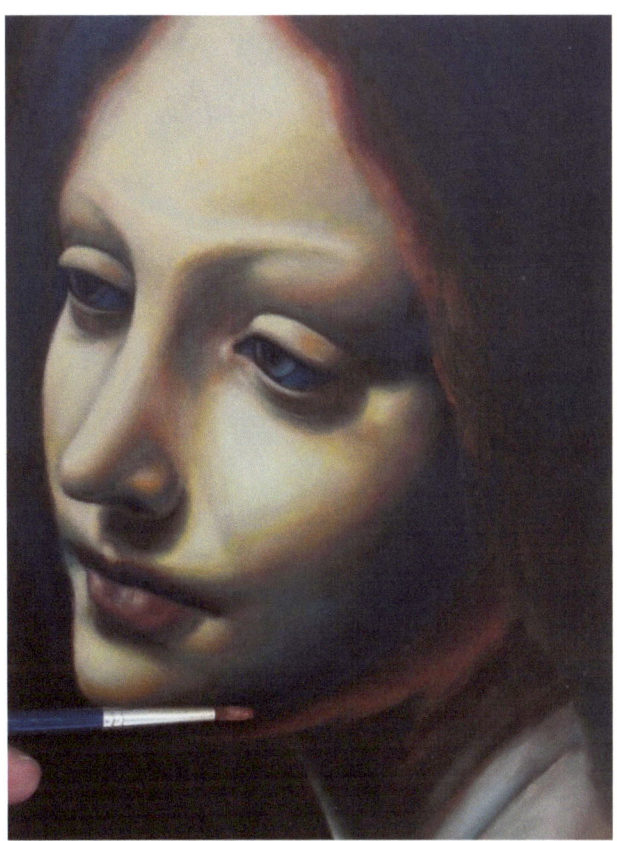

Shadows of the Mouth

39 Common misconceptions about the mouth are to be avoided when painting Da Vinci's angel. Here, very little red was used. In fact, the mouth is more about light and shadow than colour.

For the main colour, I used pthalo blue, white and a little burnt umber. A tiny amount of alizarin crimson was added to provide the blush hue. I worked the highlight colour over the lower lip, avoiding the areas reserved for shadow. The paint was applied more thinly towards the outer reaches of highlight to provide a workable paint surface on which to blend. Additional burnt umber was added in order to mute areas that appear too violet.

40 With the same sable, I applied a dusting of pthalo blue and alizarin crimson around the edges of highlight. Excess paint was wiped from the brush and I blended the seam between shadow and light.

I allowed a few ridges of shadow colour to remain in order to suggest the textures on the lower lip. Notice how the upper lip darkens towards the seam, where it meets the lower lip. But also notice the absence of outlines around the mouth. The tones are almost identical in value between the lips and the surround shadows. Softening select outlines with a clean bristle will often be necessary

An Overall View

With the facial features elaborated upon, the artist will need to stand back in order to see how one relates with the other. Watch out for imbalances. Does the shadow around the mouth parry with the shadows beneath the eyes? Is the shadow over the philtrum too heavy? Revisiting areas of the face may be necessary, which might entail softening lines and adjusting tones.

Here, I added depth to shadows across the cheekbones and chin before softening them into the jaw. Once satisfied, I put the painting away, ready for the final stage.

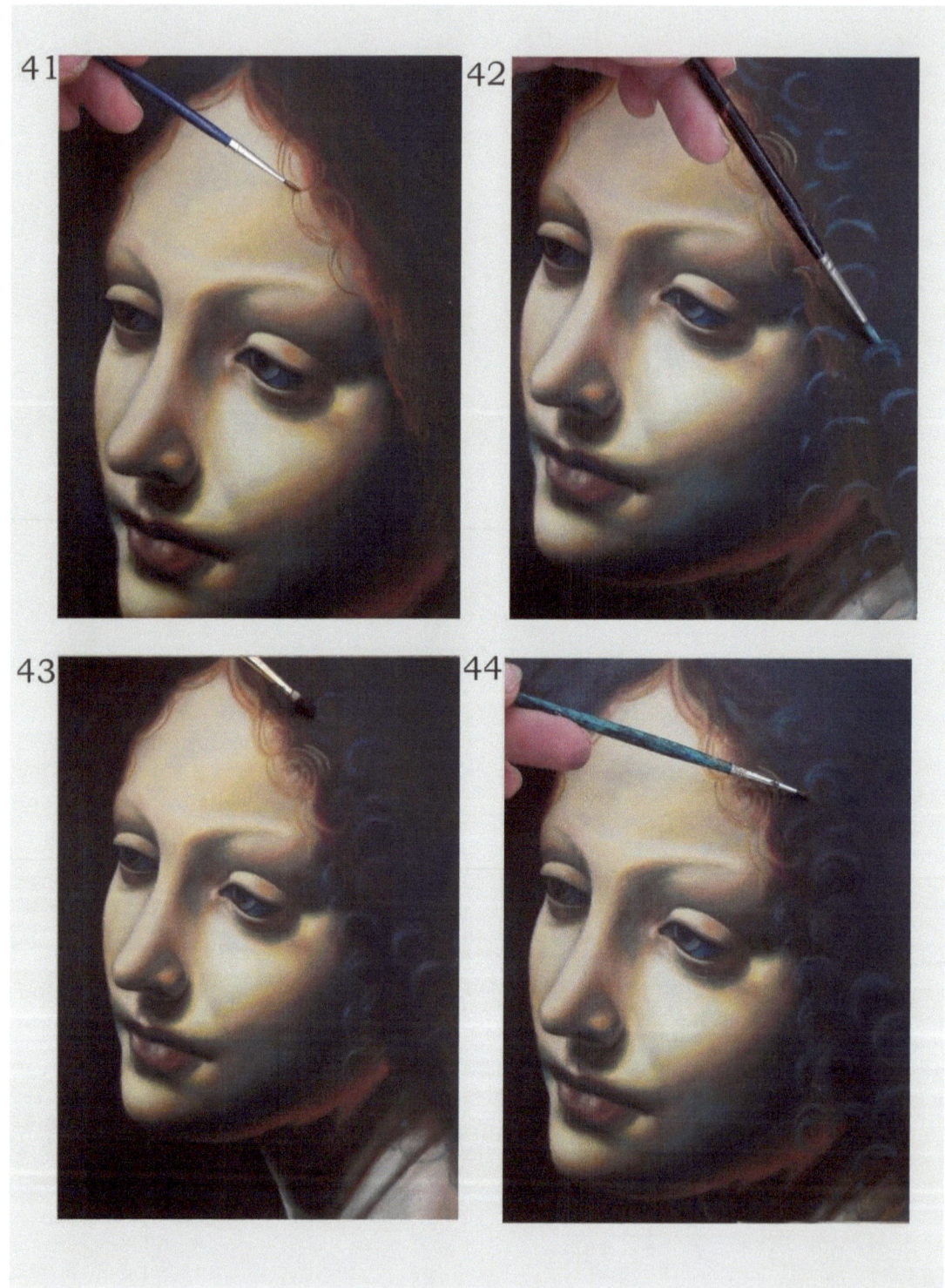

The Texture of Hair

The elements surrounding the face holds equal importance to the actual portrait as it will affect the colour cast and tonal key. A rushed background can also spoil the whole effect. This is why I would recommend completing this final stage on a separate day.

Da Vinci's treatment of the angel's hair is somewhat linear, almost illustrative. To recapture this Renaissance approach, a fine sable and a little linseed oil will be used.

41 I began with the hair strands on the angel's brow. A little burnt sienna, cadmium yellow and white was added to a fine sable, and thinned with a little linseed oil to make the paint flow. I carefully drew loose swirls around the hairline and brow to suggest curls of hair. Don't overdo the curls, but simplify. Notice three or four swirls can be seen running down the brow-bone.

Where the curls hit the light, additional cadmium yellow and white was added. Burnt sienna predominated in darker, russet areas.

42 Notice contrasting highlights in the angel's hair. Some are warm, comprising gold,

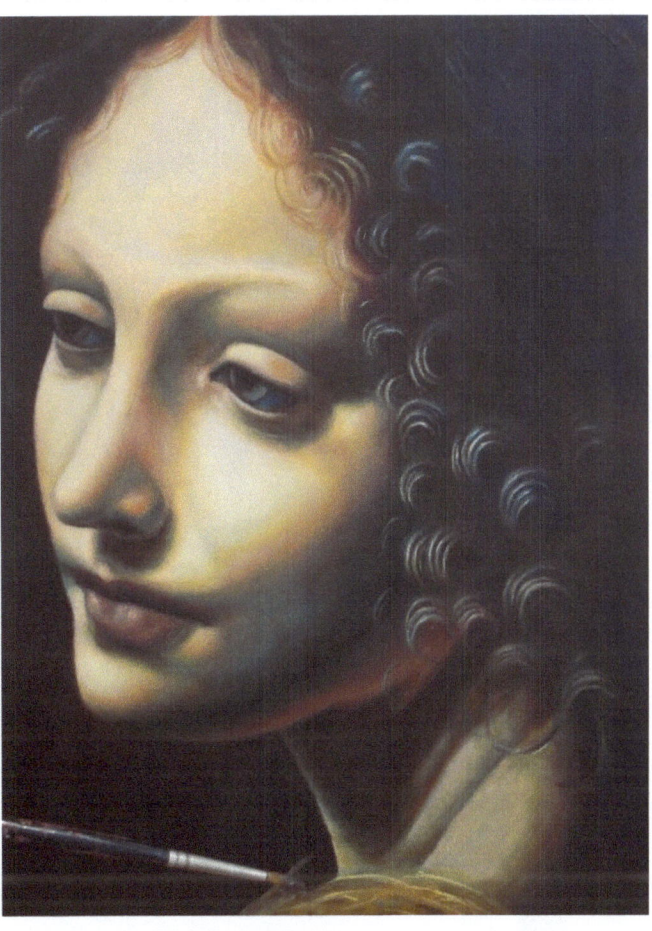

auburn and saffron; others are cool comprising of blues, greys and violets. Both bring interesting contrasts and variations against a dark background and create additional focal points. With a fine sable, I mixed pthalo blue, alizarin crimson, burnt umber and a little white, then made rudimentary swirls into the hair within shadow. Again, the paint mixture varies, so in some places more pthalo blue and alizarin crimson was used than in others. Burnt umber was introduced to bring a monochrome element to sections of hair bordering on shadow.

43 Overdoing the lines is a danger when painting hair, which could ruin the portrait. Da Vinci's rendition retains a soft, sleek feel despite the linear element. To reflect this Renaissance feel, lines too defined needs to be tempered and built on top.

Here, I went over the bluish highlights just applied with a soft bristle. I smudged out the edges into shadow. Be selective with what to smudge. Don't apply this treatment to every strand, but the sections of hair that border shadow. Smudge out also the edges of harsh lines to eradicate a 'wiry' look.

Different Coloured Strands

44 The bluish-grey highlights applied in step 42 should now appear soft and muted around the edges. Lightly smudging an area will mean lightly going over adjacent areas again. With a fine bristle, I reinstated dark sections of hair that might appear clouded after the smudging technique. Burnt umber, alizarin crimson and a little pthalo blue was dabbed around the darkest sections of hair. The angel's face now appears to really stand out against the adjacent deep shadows to bring a theatrical yet serene feel to the painting featuring *sfumato*.

39

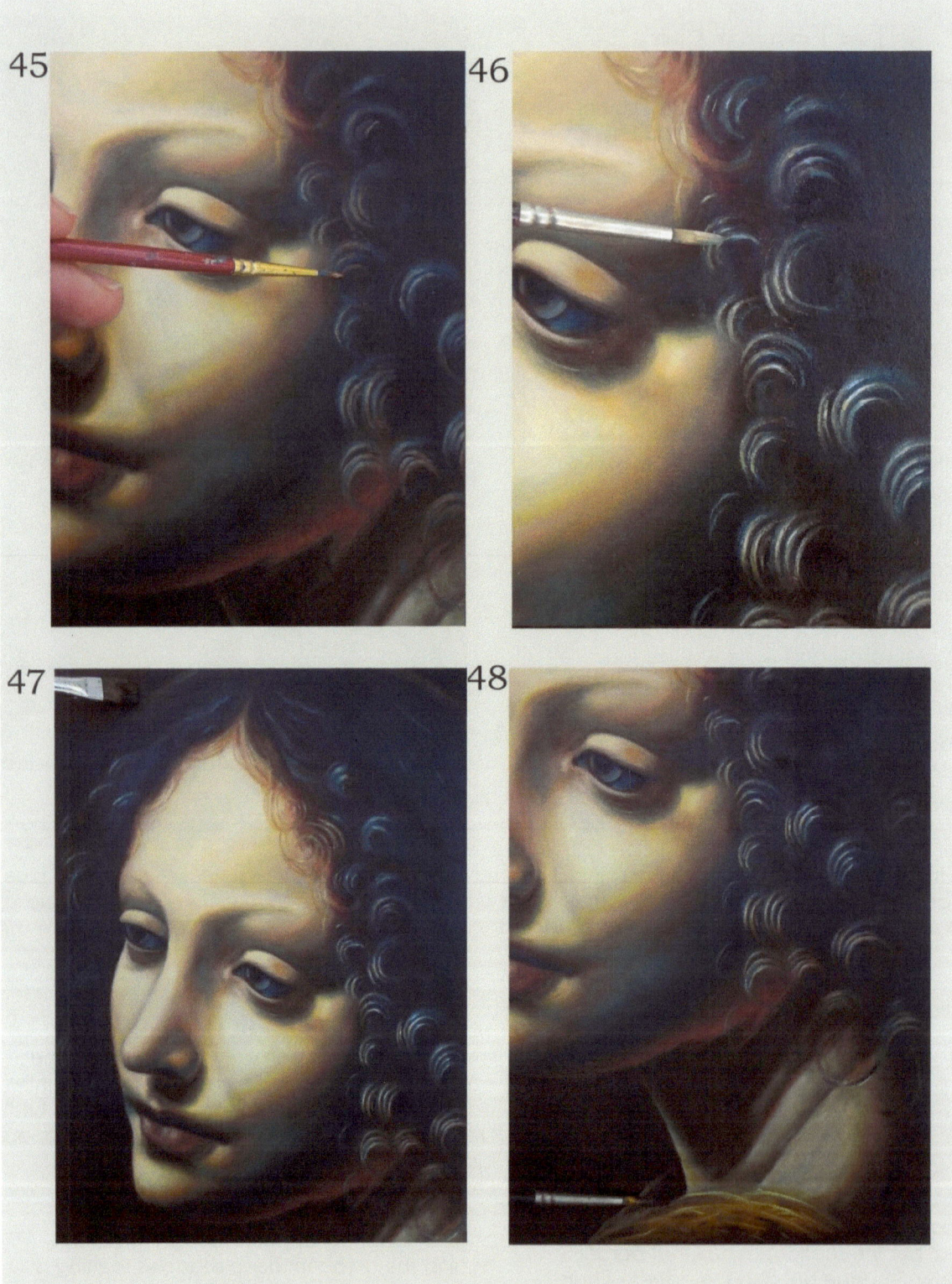

Softening Detail

45. With a fine sable, I lightly drew over the smudged lines to reinstate definition. As can be seen here, high detail can be expressed without harsh lines that could rob the focus from the angel's face.

Pthalo blue, burnt sienna and white was mixed for a soft, blue-grey. I wiped excess paint from the brush and pulled the highlights into shadow to suggest the hair catching flints of light from an overhead light source. The brightest highlight was suggested only on the leading edge of the angel's curls.

46 This close up shows colour shifts along the entire edge of each curl. Pthalo blue, burnt umber and white was applied to the highlights.

Be careful not to add too much white or the tonal key of the hair will be too heightened. As the highlight yields to shadow around each curl, more pthalo blue and alizarin crimson was added. However the under-curls yield to shadow by the addition of burnt sienna and a little cadmium yellow, to bring a silvery feel.

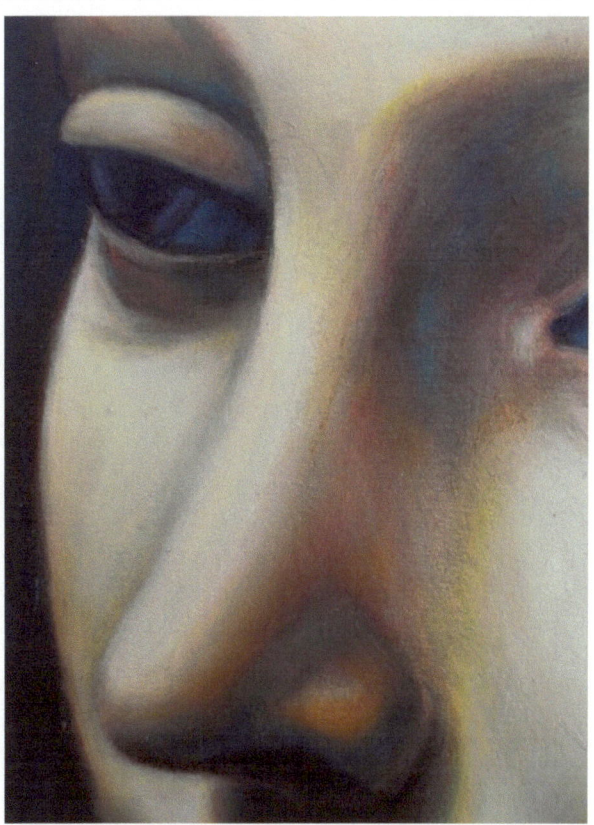

The Finishing Touches

47 As the face and hair have now received 4 oil glazes in places, the background now appears flat. With a wide bristle, I worked burnt umber and a little pthalo blue around the lower sections of the face.

As I worked the paint towards the upper section, I added a little more burnt sienna in order to suggest a soft light source. I worked a little of this dark brown colour into the dark expanse of the hair where little detail can be discerned.

As this background is similar in hue to the shadows of the face, unity is provided to the painting.

48 It may be noticed that the skin colours on the angel's neck are quite different to the face. This would seem to reflect Da Vinci's intention to retain focus upon the face. But also to inform upon the quality of light that falls upon her. Its strength would appear to steeply decline on its further reaches.

To reflect the paleness of this light, mostly pthalo blue, burnt umber and a little alizarin crimson was smudged into the pales. The neck-gear of the garment was expressed via burnt sienna, a little cadmium yellow and white via a fine sable. The colour was deepened with burnt umber towards the bottom of the painting.

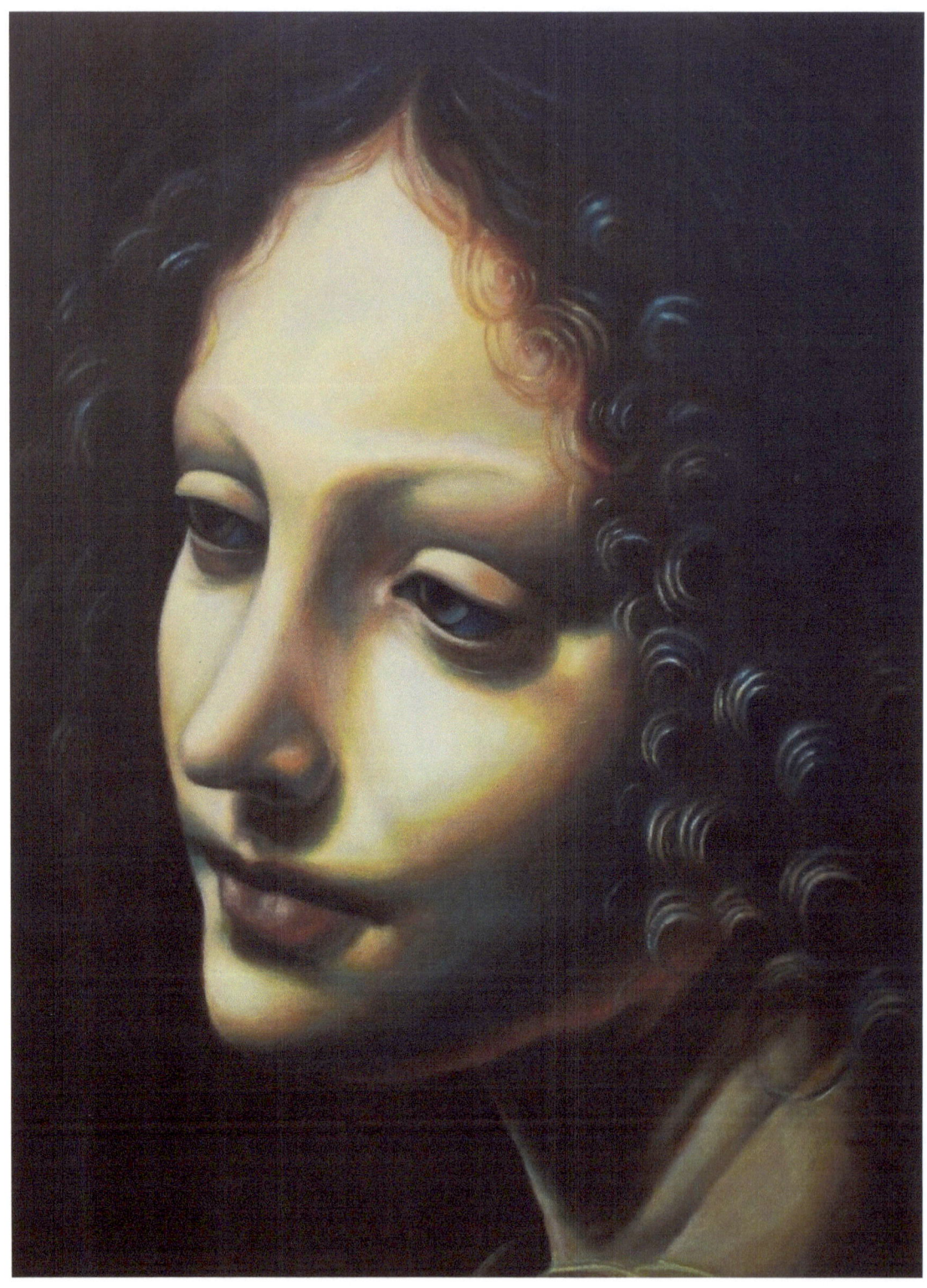

42

What went Wrong?

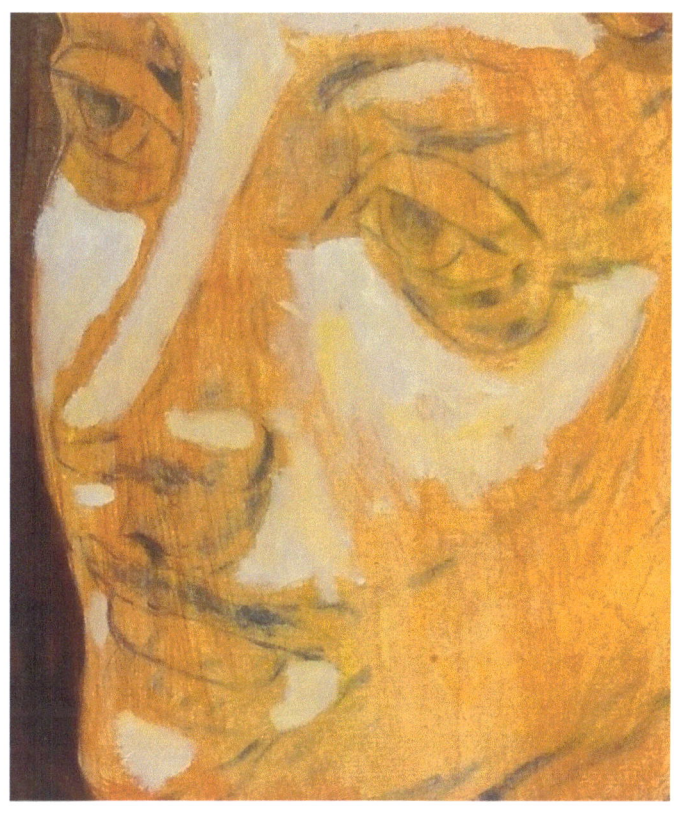

STAGE 1 OF THIS BOOK, 'the challenges ahead' is designed to forestall problems before they arise. However difficulties can still occur, which is made more likely by such a momentous project as painting Da Vinci's angel. The following advice might help.

1 Invest in good quality art materials.

Every painting begins with the art materials, which is why this point is often made. A challenging project requiring a great investment of time and energy deserves the use of artist-quality materials where it matters. This includes the art surface, the gesso, the oil paint and the art mediums. These will ensure future problems will not arise, such as cracking or sinking of the paint layer. Good quality sables will also make exacting applications such as shading and detail easier to do. However, household substitutes can be used where it doesn't matter, such as household bristles for applying the underglaze. Any non-porous material such as an old plate can be used as a mixing palette. Acrylics from any good craft store can be used in place of the branded kind.

2 Be sparing with art mediums when attaining sfumato effects.

Sfumato cannot be achieved with paint that is too runny. An oily glaze will be insufficient in covering the previous paint layer and imperfections will remain visible beneath. This means drying the brush after swilling it in artist spirits between mixes. Only a small amount of linseed oil is added in later glazes to provide flexibility to the upper paint layer. Otherwise the paint is best applied neat and blended into previously-applied colours via a soft bristle.

3 Ensure the previous glaze is dry before beginning the next.

Depending upon the atmospheric conditions, a glaze of oil paint can take up to two days to become touch-dry. Working on the next gaze before the entire painting has dried properly can cause the lifting off of some of the underlying paint as it is worked over. The result is an imperfect glaze with a patchy finish. If this is the case, gently dab excess wet paint from the art surface and leave the painting to dry properly.

4 Apply detail near the start of the painting session

Exacting processes such as illustrating the angel's eyes and the strands of hair requires a steady hand and close observation. This is why I would recommend working detail within the first hour of the painting session. Detail often forms a crucial focal point of a painting, which means it should not be rushed or undertaken when feeling tired. Use good quality sables that taper to a point for high definition.

5 Apply vibrant pigments sparingly.

Alizarin crimson, viridian green and cadmium yellow are powerful pigments which can easily dominate another colour. This means only a small amount is required to express the bands of colour where light and shadow meet, as shown in stage 4 of this book. To remedy a psychedelic-looking portrait, wipe off the erroneous colours with a dry, clean rag and reapply a fresh mix. Tone down the bright colour with a complementary or neutral colour and a little white.

6 Beware of dirty colour mixes at the juncture of two complementary colours.

As has been seen within this painting, skin tones often contain conflicting hues that lie adjacent to one another, such as blue and red. This poses the danger of dark colour bands developing where the two pigments meet. To remedy this, don't overload the brush. Apply each colour in isolation first-off via two separate sables.

Towards the juncture, apply the pigment more thinly. Then with a clean, soft brush, pull the dominant of the two colours into the more recessive. In the case of blue and russet, I would pull the blue into the russet whilst constantly wiping excess paint from the brush. A little titanium white will temper the colour mix if need be. Use small gentle strokes and keep blending.

7 Don't overload the brush with oil paint.

Working oil paint in glazes in the manner of the Renaissance style requires smooth paint layers. Troughs and ridges caused by vigorous brush marks and the application of thick paint can interfere with fine detail applied on top. Oil paint in fact can be applied in a flat, even layer without lots of art mediums. After an hour or so of oxidization, certain pigments may require a little linseed oil to help it flow.

8 Perfect blends before completing the glaze.

Perfect colour blends before putting the painting away. The tenet of allowing rough blends to remain with the view that the next glaze will conceal it, simply creates extra work for the artist. A rough blend can also show through certain colours, meaning a thicker glaze will be necessary. Treat each glaze as though to be the last, in order to bring the painting to its conclusion sooner and to save paint.

9 Work under a good light source.

A poor light source can render rough blends and colour mismatches invisible. This is because the eyes cannot perceive colours so well under poor lighting, creating a false impression of hues. Dusk and artificial light can be culprits of this problem. During the final, crucial stages of the painting involving sfumato blending and high detail, ensure the light is good. I like to work under natural light of a bright day.

10 Regularly gain distance from the painting.

Every now and then, and especially towards the end of the each glaze, stand right back from the painting. Not just a few feet, but place it against the opposite wall of a room. An image reduced in size on the visual field will look very different in appearance to close-up. Conceived niggles may seem less significant; other issues previously unnoticed may jump out. These realisations need not be acted upon immediately. Simply look at the painting and take in the overall view. Doing so can bring a clear view and a simplified plan.

Glossary

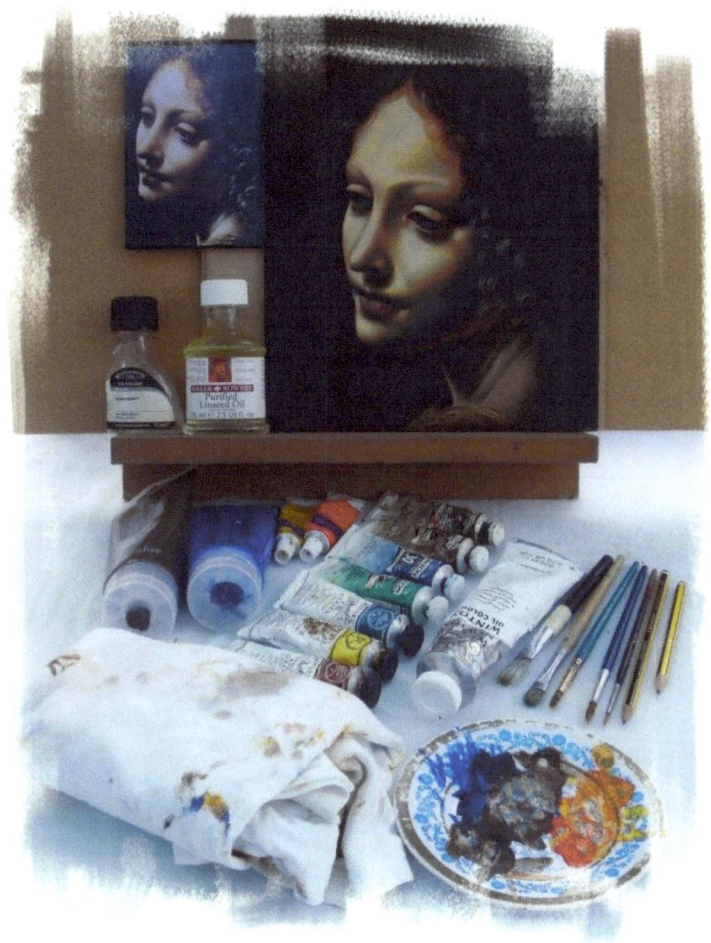

Acrylic paint: A water-soluble paint made from a polymer that dries water resistant. Unlike watercolour, opaque effects can be achieved as well as washes. Acrylic paint is useful for applying the underglaze to the oil painting.

Acrylic polymer primer: Sometimes termed 'acrylic gesso,' a water-soluble paint that dries water resistant, making it the most convenient sealant (or size) for oil painting supports such as canvases or panels. A distinction must be made from traditional gesso, which is whiting suspended in glue.

Alla prima: A painting completed in one sitting as opposed to layers.

Bristle: A stiff brush such as hog hair for robust brushwork and impasto.

Canvas: An oil painting support made from unbleached hemp or a similar fabric.

Chiaroscuro: An Italian term meaning 'light-dark'. Such an effect is found within paintings exhibiting dramatic contrasts between light and shadow.

Complementary colour: A colour situated on the opposite segment to any given colour on the colour wheel. Red, for example is the complementary to green.

Filbert: A flat bristle brush with a head that forms an oval shape.

Flat: A flat bristle brush with a head that forms a wedged shape.

Gesso: Ground white pigment suspended in glue which is applied to the painting support prior to oil painting.

Grid method: A means of scaling up (or down) a drawing by plotting points from an image overlaid with a grid onto the drawing surface possessing a similar grid of larger (or smaller) proportions.

Glaze: (In painting) a layer of paint.

Impasto: The application of thick paint.

Impasto medium: An alkyd-based medium that adds bulk to paint for impasto techniques.

Imprimatura: See underglaze.

Linseed oil: Extracted from the linseed, the carrier of oil paint. When used as a medium, it adds gloss, transparency and flow.

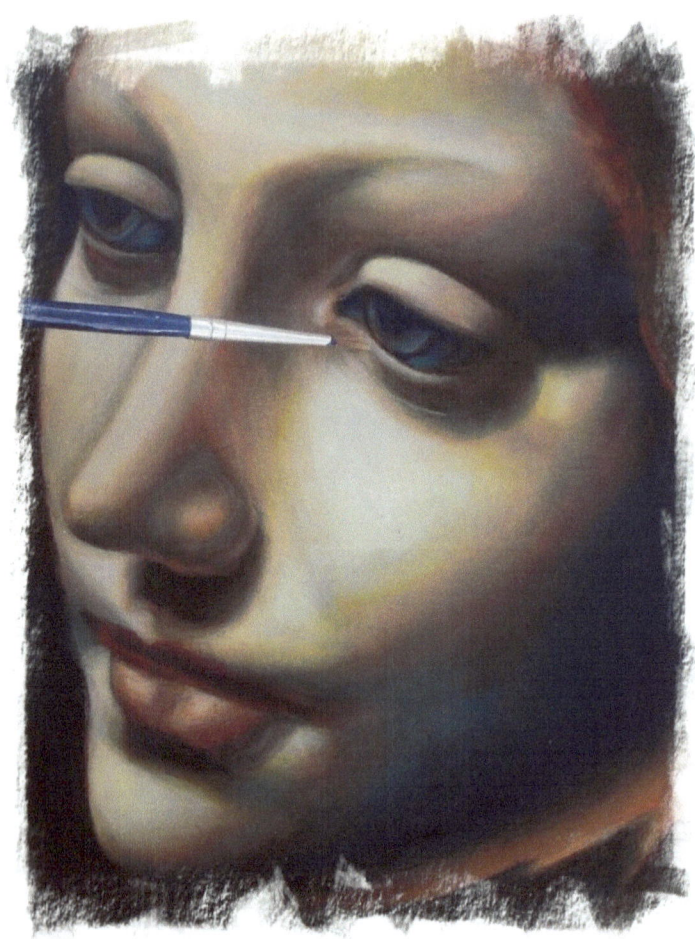

Opaque: A dense layer (of paint) that cannot be seen through.

Panel: A firm, rectangular-shaped support for oil painting, usually wood, which might be hardboard, plywood or MDF.

Round: A brush that tapers to a point for applying detail.

Sable: A soft brush made from the fur of the sable, a small mammal. A cheaper alternative is available in the form of a blend of the sable and a synthetic substitute.

Sfumato: From the Italian word *sfumare*, this means to evaporate like smoke. *Sfumato* is a chief painting practice of the Renaissance where the contours of the face are hidden in soft shadow. Leonardo da Vinci's the Mona Lisa is the most noteworthy example.

Solvent: A thinner for oil paint which is also used for cleaning the brushes. Solvents designed for artist use (not industrial) should always be used for oil painting. I use Sansador.

Support: When pertaining to oil painting, a support is the surface onto which the oil painting is applied. Suitable supports include canvas, wood, card or thick paper. The support must always be sealed with a gesso or similar sealant prior to oil painting. I use acrylic gesso primer.

Translucent: A thin layer (of paint) where detail beneath can be seen beneath.

Underdrawing: A rudimentary drawing that forms the basis of the painting.

Underglaze: sometimes known as an imprimatura, a layer of paint applied prior to the oil painting to kill the off-putting whiteness of the art surface. The underglaze can be used to add mood to the finished painting and can be any colour which might be opaque or translucent. I use acrylic paint for my underglazes.

References

The National Gallery, London Website: www.nationalgallery.org.uk

Leonardo da Vinci: The Great Artists: Their Lives, Works and Inspiration; (Marshall Cavendish Ltd, 1995)

Cole, Alison: *Colour: the Essential Visual Guide to the Art of Colour from Renaissance Painting to Modern-day Mediums;* ((Eyewitness Art in Association with the National Gallery, London, 1993)

Welton, Jude: *Looking at Paintings: the Essential Visual Guide to Understanding Paintings and their Composition;* (Eyewitness Art in Association with the National Gallery, London, 1993)

Other Books by the Author

I have practiced oil painting from the age of six and have since been involved in countless projects and commissions. A graduate from Kingston University, Surrey and with a PCET teaching qualification from Warwick University, I have won competitions, taught life drawing and have written numerous articles on teaching art.

An overview of all the following books can be found and purchased on my Oil Painting Medic Blog.

Art Books (Select books available on Kindle, small & large Edition)

Why do My Clouds Look like Cotton Wool? – Plus 25 Solutions to Other Landscape Painting Peeves

Why do My Ellipses Look like Doughnuts? – Plus 25 Solutions to Other Still Life Painting Peeves

Why do My Skin Tones look Lifeless? – Plus s 25 Solutions to Other Portrait Painting Peeves

The Ultimate Oil Painting Solution: for Landscape Art, Portraiture and Still Life

Landscape Painting in Oils: 20 Step by Step Guides

The Artist's Garden in Oils: 18 Step by Step Guides

Portrait Painting in Oil: 10 Step by Step Guides from Old Masters

Skin Tones in Oil: 10 Step by Step Guides from Old Masters

Oil Painting the Mona Lisa in Sfumato: a Portrait Painting Challenge in 48 Steps

Oil Painting the Angel within Da Vinci's the Virgin of the Rocks: Unleash the Right Brain to Paint the Three-quarter Portrait View

How Can I Inspire my Painting Class? (Lesson Plan Ideas for Oil Painting in Post Compulsory Education & an Essential Guide to Teaching)

Draw What You See Not What You Think You See

Oil Paintings from Your Garden GMC Publications Ltd

Oil Paintings from the Landscape GMC Publications Ltd

Illustrated Children's Books

Katie's Magic Teapot and the Cosmic Pandas

Katie and the Cosmic Pandas' Deep Sea Voyage

Katie's Magic Teapot Omnibus Edition

Ben's Little Big Adventure

www.ingramcontent.com/pod-product-compliance
Lightning Source LLC
Chambersburg PA
CBHW040751200526
45159CB00025B/1840